Sensational '60s

Wheels of Change

Edited by John A. Gunnell

Published by

krause
publications

700 E. State Street • Iola, WI 54990-0001

Library of Congress Catalog Number: 93-80694
ISBN: 0-87341-294-X
Printed in the United States of America

Contents

Acknowledgements

The '60s were really a trip for me. Jalopy stock car races, walks on Emerson Hill, ferry rides, Yankee games, Brooklyn Tech, Staten Island Community College, Bohack, Beech-Nut, W.T. Grant's, blackouts, black power, water shortages, JFK, LBJ, '55 Chevys, the Corner Shop, the Community Center, marriage, Suzy and John and lots more.

Sincere thanks go to the whole gang that lived with me through the '60s, including Bruce, Chico, Gail, Georgie, Jo Ann, Johnny and Gerry, Jose, "Lucarino," Mary Ellen, Melvin, Mike and Judy, "Pepsi," Stuie, Tony and Vinnie. Most of all, thanks to my wife, Kitch, who I "asked out" in 1963 and still live with today.

Introduction

As we all know, the '60s were a tumultuous time for the United States. Demonstrations, assassinations, riots and confrontations, disasters and tragedies dotted the decade. This book touches on all of these, but not to the depths of other works that we've enjoyed such as "Life in the '60s" and "Keep Your Eyes on the Prize."

Instead, this is a book that views the decade by associating photos of products, mainly automobiles, with facts ... trivia, if you will ... from the 1960s. In many cases, the facts relate to population statistics, sports, hobbies, government agencies and historical news items. They may not capture the terror caused by whistling bullets, the stress of the struggle for human rights or the hot flames of burning ghettos. Still, they do tell us much about the era; perhaps even some things we've not heard before.

For example, did you know that surfing and ballooning grew popular in the '60s because of technological changes? Were you aware that the motorhome boom that occurred in the '60s was the outgrowth of a housing shortage in the '50s? These facts never made headlines, but they do reveal some interesting aspects of life 25-35 years ago. We lived through the '60s and, still, in researching the book, we found out many things that we didn't know.

Such things are important. History books are filled with events that we read about in newspapers, but which have very little impact on our daily lives. That's one reason why the associative nature of this book works so well. In scrambling to find facts to "fit" a certain photo, we often stumble upon fragments of yesteryear that would have much lower priority in a more scholarly study.

We must warn you that a liberal amount of "artistic license" has been employed to tie some of the car photos into factual associations. In other words, there are cases where we "stretched" connections a bit to make things work. This was done with tongue planted firmly in cheek and a robust sense of humor. Please take it that way. We did not stretch the facts themselves.

Also, be warned that the pup seen in a photo with a caption about dog show winners, is probably not the show dog. Likewise, the rubber raft in the back of a Chevrolet pickup did not win the *America's Cup*. We simply linked the dog, raft or other item with some obtainable and loosely associated information. Sounds like fun, doesn't it?

There are non-automotive photos in the book. They are inset photos showing products (or in some cases people) that tell us even more about the decade. We call them our "windows on the '60s."

Fun is the sole purpose for putting this book together. As a '60s car enthusiast, you'll love the photos of convertibles, wagons, Sport Coupes and other cars, plus trucks and motorcycles. The captions will fill you in on your favorite era and they may help you if you're playing "Trivial Pursuit."

John A. Gunnell

April, 1994

Change for the Fun of It

Yearly Improvements Marked 1960s Cars

The "Sensational '60s" were a bridge between the "Fabulous '50s" and the "Senseless '70s." Automobiles of the early 1960s still had the innocent charm of the 1950s. They were flashy, fast and foolish. Changes would come, during the decade, in technology, styling and marketing. Most would be improvements.

In a real way, the '60s car represented the ultimate '50s machine; the postwar car refined to a high state of purity and perfection. Until the "ground rules" changed, Detroit was set on a course of stabile prices, consistent improvement and better business year after year.

Automobiles of the early 1960s still had the innocent charm of the 1950s. They were flashy, fast and foolish.

Except for 1961, when the industry over-reacted to an economic "hiccup," production climbed steadily from 1960 to 1966. Sales were strong because the products were exciting and prices seemed affordable and fair. There was constantly something new to desire in styling, features, engineering or performance and it was just as likely to cost less or the same as last year, as it was to cost a few dollars more.

Even as the clouds of war darkened in Southeast Asia, sales and production sustained themselves near their peak. In the final three years of the decade, business tapered off, but not as much as one may suspect. Despite a period of war, labor unrest, tight money, high interest rates and domestic turmoil, the industry's third best year was 1969 and 1968 was fourth best. This was nothing short of amazing.

Outside influences upset the apple cart. Left on its own, chances are good that Detroit would have sailed through the '70s and '80s, building on the '60s, just as this decade built on the '50s. This, however, was not to be. Greed, government meddling and the inability to create excitement in a non-creative atmosphere brought the auto industry to its knees soon after the '60s ended.

While they were here, the '60s were a great era. The cars of that decade were fun to look at, fun to listen to, fun to drive. As machines, they were darn near perfect. Changes were made for the fun of it, not because anything was basically wrong with the product. Maybe that's why 1960s cars provide so much fun to collectors today.

Here's a brief, year-by-year rundown of what happened in the new-car industry during the Sensational '60s ... the "Wheels of Change" years.

America's 1960 compacts changed the automobile marketplace. They bowed in the fall of 1959 as 1960 models and included the Chevrolet Corvair.

The three-year-old Edsel was dropped. Only about 100,000 had been sold in that period.

Studebaker's Lark was already out. It helped the Studebaker-Packard name survive a few more years.

1960

America's 1960 compacts changed the automobile marketplace. They bowed in the fall of 1959 as 1960 models and included the Chevrolet Corvair, the Ford Falcon, the Mercury Comet and the Valiant from Chrysler. The latter would become a Plymouth, but wasn't, yet.

Studebaker's Lark was already out. It helped the Studebaker-Packard name survive a few more years. American Motors also did well with its Rambler. Imported car sales started sliding, in face of the new competition.

The three-year-old Edsel was dropped. Only about 100,000 had been sold. Chevrolet outdistanced Ford in model-year production. In the Chrysler stable, Dodge dealers got the Dart and no longer needed a Plymouth franchise to satisfy entry-level buyers.

A lengthy steel strike impacted the industry to the tune of 700,000 cars and trucks not produced. This business was lost. General Motors was hurt the worst. However, use of aluminum in building cars went up. Its production was more than double that of 1950. Grilles, wheel covers and other parts were stamped from the lightweight metal. By 1961, even aluminum engines would be seen.

Interestingly, six-cylinder engines saw revived popularity in 1960. They accounted for more than half of all new-car power plants. This was part of a "retraction-reaction" to America's late-1957 recession. That economic "blip" temporarily popularized imported cars and brought the American compacts on-stream.

Despite the 116-day steel strike, factory sales of passenger cars rose 19 percent in 1960. They stood at 6.74 million. Truck sales also rose to 1.21 million. It was the auto industry's third largest production year ever. Model-year output peaked at just over six million units.

Three out of four Americans ... in 39.5 million families ... owned automobiles. About seven million families had more than one. And 85 million Americans were licensed to drive. Cars contributed $10.5 billion to the domestic economy in special taxes alone.

1961

In another change-filled year, the American automobile industry hit one million new-cars in dealer inventories for the first time in 1961. The five big car makers ... General Motors, Ford, Chrysler, American Motors and Studebaker ... all posted a profitable year. In the fall, the DeSoto disappeared. Over two million had been made since the marque's launch in 1928.

Chevrolet remained the number one automaker. Ford retained second. Pontiac slipped into third place in calendar-year sales, but American Motors *built* more 1961 models. Ford and Chevrolet introduced new cast iron engines, so the trend towards aluminum was by no means cast in stone. There was a shake out in imported car registrations and foreign automakers began to cut prices.

Pontiac slipped into third place in 1961 calendar-year sales, but American Motors built more 1961 models.

There was a shake out in 1961 imported car registrations and foreign automakers began to cut prices.

Remaining conscious of the late-1950s trend towards value-oriented buyers, the industry introduced sealed "lifetime" chassis lubrication, ceramic-armored exhaust systems, self-adjusting brakes and extended lubrication in 1961. There was a big push, at this time, to eliminate transmission "humps." Pontiac placed the Tempest's transmission at the rear.

Buick (Special), Oldsmobile (F-85), Pontiac (Tempest) and Dodge (Lancer) issued new compact models. Aluminum engines were standard or optional in many compacts. In the spring, luxury edition compacts came out from General Motors (Buick Skylark, F-85 Cutlass, Tempest LeMans) and Ford (Falcon Futura, Comet S-22).

In July of 1961, Chrysler got a new president, following a scandal involving kickbacks from suppliers.

Factory passenger car sales slipped 16 percent to 5.55 million, but truck sales were down just slightly. Exports dropped, to 337,000, from 360,000 the year before. Model-year production stood at 5.4 million. The total number of automobile registrations was a record 76 million.

1962

Where were you in '62? asked the ads for "American Graffiti." This was a year that set the pace for the next 10 in the car business. The youth market had arrived. Fast and fiery changes were coming.

Sporty GT models and a wide range of engine options characterized 1962. Buick had a new V-6. Other power plants ranged from the Falcon's 85-horsepower inline six to optional Ford and Chrysler V-8s with over 400 horsepower. However, average maximum horsepower actually dropped from a 1959 high of 270 horsepower down to 228. Some observers predicted that the horsepower race was over. Little did they know what was coming!

Cars were generally lower, wider and airier. They had an average of 15 percent more glass area. Braking and handling had improved greatly from a few years earlier. Fins, chrome and two-tone paint were starting to fade away. General Motors came out with a hardtop that looked like a ragtop. It was a winner.

A new class of automobiles, the intermediate, bowed in 1962. These mid-size models included the Chevy II Nova, the Ford Fairlane and the Mercury Meteor. The economy had bounced back, though, and many buyers wanted big cars to go with their big new salaries. The change came so suddenly that Dodge revived its 122-inch wheelbase Custom 880, only four months after phasing it out.

Others, like Plymouth and American Motors (Ambassador), got caught with "smaller" full-size cars that few wanted by the time they came out. They were strong, handsome machines, but "biting-the-bullet" was passe ... at least for a while. Cadillac issued a short deck model for San Francisco dowagers who had small, tight garages. It didn't sell. Pontiac was lucky, it upped its wheelbase to 120 inches at just the right time, protecting its new third rank in industry production.

Changes in buyer preferences came so suddenly that Dodge revived its 122-inch wheelbase Custom 880, in 1962, only four months after phasing it out.

There was little change in the imported car field, except for the addition of quad headlamps to the Rolls-Royce. As usual, the British luxury marque was five years behind times. Volkswagen made noise about its conventional new "Squareback" model, but continued to sell Beetles as if they were going out of style. Other import makers were not having similar luck.

Drag racing between Ford, Chevrolet, Dodge, Plymouth, Pontiac and Mercury re-accelerated the horsepower derby. Special, supposedly-for-racing-only, engines were growing to more than 400 cubic inches and pushing out over 450 "ponies." Terms like hemi, Super Sport (SS), Super-Duty, Super Stock and Ram Charger generated youthful excitement. High-performance would dominate the decade from 1962 on.

Calendar-year sales went to 6.8 million cars and 1.2 million trucks in 1962. The more-important-to-collectors model-year production was also up at 6.69 million. Registrations, special tax dollars and other numbers generated by automaking all increased modestly, but the number of licensed American drivers zoomed to 90.5 million level.

In 1962, Plymouth got caught with "smaller" full-size cars that few buyers wanted by the time they came out.

1963

Many of 1963's changes were "firsts." Three completely new sports/personal cars were seen: the Buick Riviera, the Studebaker Avanti; and the Corvette Sting Ray. The last two had fiberglass bodies and offered optional disk brakes. You could get fuel-injection on the Corvette again, while the Avanti had a supercharger available. All three had bucket seats, a floor shift and a center console. The Riviera had a glued-in rear window. The Corvette had retractable headlamps. (Do you get the idea they were trying to out-do each other?)

Chrysler handed out 50 turbine-engined prototypes to selected drivers across the nation, asking them to test the cars in real-life conditions.

General Motors introduced the Tilt-Away steering wheel. Chevrolet issued a "straight" six with seven main bearings. Ford brought out the first fully-synchronized three-speed manual transmission. Ramblers had doors made of galvanized steel. Cadillac introduced a five-joint drive shaft to fight the "battle of the (transmission) bulge." Chrysler products used alternators. Aware of what was coming, Detroit installed seat belt anchors in cars and said that front seat belts would be added on January 1, 1964.

Cast iron engines won renewed popularity. Pontiac dropped its lightweight Tempest V-8 (sourced from Oldsmobile) and Chrysler dropped its aluminum slant six. Most motors had more compression, multi-barrel carburetors and generally more oomph. The 50,000-mile warranty was Chrysler's new sales tool. Having owned a '63 Chrysler, I can tell you they didn't have to worry about excessive warranty claims. They were great cars and many still exist.

Ford renounced the American Automobile Manufacturers Association's "racing ban" and launched its "Total Performance" campaign with a *Thunderbolt*. (That's what they called the Fairlane with a 427-cubic-inch V-8 stuffed into it.) Soon, Chrysler countered with the "*Street Hemi*" and the "factory muscle car" era was coming 'round the corner.

Unnoticed by many, Honda, in far away Japan, put a handsome little roadster into production and said they were going Grand Prix racing. Meanwhile, the company started to market motor bikes and small motorcycles here. These revolutionized the two-wheeler industry and sold very well. The "sleeping giants" of Detroit, though, were more afraid of Volkswagen and others. Renault's business zoomed 15 percent in early 1963. Britain built five of every six sports cars sold here. Mercedes-Benz introduced a $23,000 Pullman limousine. In contrast, Japan wasn't viewed as a major threat. Later, it would become one, but not in the '60s.

As an experiment, Chrysler handed out 50 turbine-engined prototypes to selected drivers across the nation, asking them to test the cars under real-life conditions. A complete analysis of test results was nation, asking them to test the cars under real-life conditions. A complete analysis of test results was published in booklet form and, though it sounded positive, turbine cars were not produced.

12

More than half the world's existing cars were American models in 1963. Domestic market new-car production hit a record 7.34 million 1963 models. With buses and trucks added, the total was nine million. Some 43 million families here owned cars and 8.7 million had at least one extra vehicle.

1964

Changes for the good and bad came in 1964, a year that began with record six-month sales of 4.43 million cars and wound up with model-year production of 7.89 million. Sales were counted above eight million, an all-time record.

First some good news: Ford released its new Mustang (technically a 1965 model), at the New York World's Fair, in April. It came out about two weeks after the Plymouth Barracuda bowed and wound up being the best-selling new-car in history.

Next the bad news: After building 33,150 vehicles, Studebaker stopped manufacturing in the United States. It continued limited production in Canada. Meanwhile, General Motors was hurt by a massive strike.

The "big car" look was a winner in 1964. Some small economy models grew into "senior" compacts. Chevrolet had a new mid-size Chevelle. Pontiac pushed full-size performance with a new 2 + 2 Catalina.

Chryslers got new roof lines, Ramblers got a new seven-main-bearing engine, up-market General Motors wagons got "vista roofs" and Cadillacs got a 429-cubic-inch engine. Oldsmobile introduced its Jetstar 88 and Jetstar I, while Mercury dropped its Meteor line.

The new Mustang, with options ranging from grocery-getter to race car, took off like a rocket. The Chevrolet Impala SS was picking up followers and Ford's Galaxie 500XL was a crowd-puller.

Average engine size was up again, to 287 cubic inches. Oldsmobile introduced a thin-wall V-8. The Corvair got more air-cooled cubic inches. Then General Motors told its divisions to stop racing. Ford continued in the other direction, rolling out its "Total Performance" push.

Several "new-and-improved" automatic transmissions came out. A few were considered "lemons" when new, though today's collectors say the reputation was undeserved. Automatics were found in 75 percent of full-size cars. Seventy-three percent had V-8s.

A world market for cars was starting to evolve. Over one-third of Ford's early-year 1964 production went overseas.

A world market for cars was starting to evolve. Over one-third of Ford's early-year production went overseas. Chrysler exported 30.5 percent and General Motors 23.2 percent. There were 158.4 million cars around the globe, 12.2 million more than in 1963. In the United States, every 2.9 people owned one car. For other nations the ratio was different: 8.4 for England, 10.4 for Germany, 20.8 for Italy and 140.09 for Japan. The world average was one car for 28.5 people.

Fourth quarter United Auto Workers strikes cost General Motors 550,000 sales. Ford and American Motors also lost some business, along with Mack Truck and White. These truck firms were also caught up in government anti-trust actions.

1965

Styling changes. That was 1965's big automotive contribution. General Motors cars showcased the Buick Riviera-inspired "Coke bottle" shape. Chrysler and Ford went more towards the Mustang's crisp, angular visage.

Big cars seemed to get the most revisions from all manufacturers. I remember a friend buying one of the first Impala fastbacks and causing quite a stir with it. I myself fell in love with the prow-noses depicted in Pontiac's lavish 1965 sales booklets. Later, I used and abused a 1965 Ford Custom 500 "company car." I loved it for the two years I drove it. Chevrolet got a luxurious new Caprice Custom Sedan option package.

Other than the first Mustang fastback and an all-new (and great-looking) Corvair, most small- and mid-sized 1965 cars were merely face-lifted. Redesigned cars generally got new curved glass side windows. Cadillacs (finally) lost their tailfins.

The first factory AM/FM radios appeared in 1965. Chrysler's push-button gear shift disappeared. Some 10 models got new disk brakes. Cadillac added a tilt-and-telescope steering wheel. Roomier perimeter frames and longer wheelbases were used. Tires had a lower profile. Oldsmobile went to a larger (425 cubic inch), but lighter in weight engine.

With General Motors out of racing, FoMoCo and MoPar drivers went at it with a passion. Plymouths ran one, two, three at the Daytona 500, while Ford headed off for the Grand Prix circuits of Europe. In drag racing, the dominant force was a toss up.

With prices climbing only a fraction of a percent and a healthy economy, rosy sales projections proved on-the-money and model-year production soared to 8.84 million cars. That was a million more than ever before!

Styling changes were 1965's big contribution. General Motors cars showcased the 1963 Buick Riviera-inspired "Coke bottle" shape.

Chevrolet was first. Ford was second (and over two million for the first time in a model-year). Pontiac was third again; more than double the not-so-long-ago leader American Motors.

When 1965 ended, there were nearly 75 million cars and 15 million trucks registered in America. The industry saw net sales come in around $35 billion. General Motors made $1.54 billion, Ford made $540 million and Chrysler earned a profit of $136 million. Even Studebaker pulled in $8 million. Only American Motors was a loser, with $13 million in red ink.

1966

A really big "sports car" was 1966's really big change. This Oldsmobile Toronado had an sleek body with hide-away headlights, a massive V-8 and front-wheel-drive. Shades of Cord's 810/812 model of the 1930s!

Most other full-size cars, except Lincolns and Rivieras, were only face-lifted and refined. The Caprice nameplate now adorned a new Chevrolet top-of-the-line series. Among mid-sizes, the Dodge Coronet; Plymouth Belvedere; Ford Fairlane; Comet; and F-85 were restyled. The Pontiac Tempest and Chevrolet Chevelle both had smoother, rounder sheet metal, with an overhead cam six for the Tempest. The compact Chevy II got bigger and more stylish.

The 1966 Oldsmobile Toronado had a sleek body with hide-away headlights, a massive V-8 and front-wheel-drive. Shades of the Cord 810/812 model of the 1930s!

Seven safety items were added to all cars. Lincolns got a standard 462-cubic-inch engine. Most cars offered optional eight-track tape players. There was much emphasis placed on extras, which added 38 to 40 percent more to prices of the average vehicle. That ran the cost of the average $2,300 compact above $3,100 and boosted a $5,400 big car to nearly $7,500.

The year saw uneven business, with sales zooming in the first half and slowing down late in the year. This was somewhat related to a heightened war effort in Vietnam. I recall a friend purchasing a new 1966 GTO, before he went to Southeast Asia. He never had the opportunity to take it out again.

By late summer, model-year production stood at a very respectable 8.61 million cars. However, profits were down for all companies, except Studebaker (which made $8.3 million after phasing out auto production) and American Motors, (which *Lost* $4 million less).

Four out of five households now owned a car. Multi-car families totaled 12 million. Two out of three adults were licensed to drive. Cars were said to affect 800,000 businesses employing 12 million workers. They consumed 75 million gallons of gasoline.

On September 9, 1966, President Lyndon Baines Johnson signed the Traffic Safety Act of 1966 into law. It set forth equipment mandates for all vehicles and gave the federal government authority to influence the design and equipment of motor vehicles sold in the United States.

1967

Heavy styling changes for compacts and 17 new safety standards headlined changes in 1967 American automobiles. This year also marked the beginning of "sticker shock," as prices leapt (for the first time in a while) by a substantial 2.1 percent. The government verified that the average increase of $55 was justified by the safety equipment, but in retrospect, we can see that this hike started an ongoing trend.

There was a bevy of all-new or re-engineered models, including a front-wheel-drive Cadillac Eldorado, the Chevrolet Camaro and Pontiac Firebird (General Motor's Mustang fighters), the Mercury Cougar, a bigger AMC Marlin and a Barracuda with three different roof lines. Chrysler's Imperial went to a unitized body, while the Thunderbird went the other way.

American Motors had new 290- and 343-cubic-inch V-8s; Buick had new 401- and 430-cubic-inch V-8s; and the Camaro was first to use the now-so-familiar 350-cubic-inch V-8. Chrysler added a 318-cubic-inch motor and Pontiac bumped its 389-cubic-inch "big-block" to 400 cubic inches.

Ford's Fairlane had a Cruise-O-Matic transmission that shifted manually or automatically. Automatic air-leveling was seen on more upscale General Motors products, while Pontiac introduced recessed windshield wipers. The Thunderbird featured ventless side glass. Most cars had bigger, safer tires.

At the beginning of model-year 1967, industry projections were for another nine million unit year. The cars were introduced about two weeks earlier than usual, to extend the selling period. In addition, warranty coverage was improved.

Chrysler, which launched the five-year/50,000 mile drive train warranty in 1963, now doubled its coverage on the 1967 cars to two years or 24,000 miles. The other automakers followed its lead.

Chrysler, which launched the five-year/50,000 mile drive train warranty in 1963, now doubled its coverage on the rest of the car, to two years or 24,000 miles. The other automakers followed its lead. Ford even added a drive train warranty for used cars, back to 1964 models, on a share-the-cost basis.

Initial reactions to the annual styling changes and warranty and safety improvements were positive. By the end of the model-year, however, production fell by about a million units. It stood at 7.66 million.

1968

The auto market rebounded in 1968 and model-year production peaked at 8.4 million cars. That was in spite of a Ford strike that started off the year and cost the company 100,000 production units. Most mid-size cars got changed styling and American Motors fans got a hot two-seat sports car called the AMX.

One of the year's unusual changes was seen in General Motor's intermediates. The two-doors had a shorter wheelbase than four-doors. The purpose was to give sportier models the popular long hood/short deck look. Dodge's Charger was sleeked up very nicely and, in the spring, Lincoln gave "premature" birth to its 1969 Continental Mark III.

Prices for the new models were up an average of $100 or three percent. It was the industry's third consecutive hike and the largest in nearly 10 years. This was a big year for appearance revisions. The automakers spent $1.5 billion, the most since 1965, to bring in the new models. There were some very exciting changes.

The Corvette was renamed Stingray (instead of Sting Ray). Its appearance changes were much more extensive than the name modification. Patterned after an exotic-looking Mako Shark show car, the all-new-for 1968 sports car was curvaceous and clean.

Other cars with major revamps included the Chevy II, Dodge Charger, Oldsmobile F-85, Fairlane, Dodge Coronet and Plymouth Belvedere. The Comet had a new look and a new name (Montego) on some editions. The Pontiac Tempest/LeMans/GTO group got a new integrated bumper/grille. Cadillac went to a 472-cubic-inch engine.

A special Hurst/Olds was brought to market as a joint effort of Oldsmobile and an outside modification firm. It was the first in a line of rare, semi-aftermarket, high-performance cars that are very collectible now.

Options continued to sell very well. Optional transmissions were featured in over 90 percent of all cars. Nearly 40 percent had air conditioning. V-8s were installed in 85 percent. Bucket seats were found in 24 percent and 23 percent wore vinyl tops.

General Motors added the steering wheel buzzer that we hated then and still do now. Ford adapted the collapsible steering column, catching up with the other manufacturers, who had done so in 1967. Warranties and safety were both enhanced again. The government started listing recall campaigns.

The auto market rebounded in 1968 and model-year production peaked at 8.4 million cars. That was in spite of a Ford strike that started off the year and cost the company 100,000 units.

The big changes swung back to the big cars in 1969. The Plymouth Fury had new "fuselage" styling, said to be aircraft-inspired.

1969

Big changes swung back to big cars in 1969. The Plymouth Fury, Dodge Polara and Monaco and Chrysler Imperial all received new "fuselage" styling, said to be aircraft-inspired. The full-size Fords and Mercuries were redesigned. Chevrolet had a new appearance. Big Buicks and the AMC Ambassador rode on longer wheelbases.

Also restyled was the Mustang and the Camaro/Firebird body. At midyear, the limited-edition Z-28 and Trans Am high-performance options were added for the latter pair. The GTO received a soft "Endura" rubber-like front end that was purposeful-looking and damage-resistant.

Warranty coverage was reduced, but not for original owners. Side-marker lights were a newly required safety item. On January 1, 1969, front seat headrests became standard equipment on all cars. That brought a price hike above the $50 to $55 added at fall introduction time. Fords and Chryslers got recessed wipers and more cars of all brands adopted ventless side windows. Anti-skid braking was available on the Thunderbird and Continental Mark III. General Motors cars got guard rail-like steel beams inside their doors to add to their impact resistance.

Pontiac claimed that its restyled and re-engineered Grand Prix had the longest snout ever seen in the car industry, but I don't know if they bothered to measure the Bugatti Royale's hood. There was a hot SJ model that prompted advertising copywriters to mention the Duesenberg.

New-for-1969 options included headlight washers on Chevrolets, a new three-speed Turbo-Hydra-matic transmission, a "Big Six" from Ford (250 cubic inches), electrically heated rear windows and in-the-windshield radio antennas.

The model-year production total for 1969 hit 8.44 million cars. It was the third best year in the history of the industry. All in all, the 1960s were kind to Detroit, but that would change during the next decade.

The 1969 Lincoln Continental Mark III had grille styling inspired by classic old cars combined with advanced technical features.

The '60s reflected in
U.S. Steel ads

. . . and that's you!

Today's (US) steels lighten your work . . . brighten your leisure . . . widen your world.

Steel is for setting the style

Look at this lineup for 1960! Sleek cars and saucy cars, cars that say "style" in every line—and every one sculptured in modern steels. Strong, versatile new steels let designers create curves and sweeping lines that once were impossible. Stainless Steel trim *stays* bright. New steels set the pace for driving fun. Working parts are practically indestructible when they're made from strong, hard steels. See your dealer soon—start the 60's in style with a new car!

(US) **United States Steel**

Lightens
your work

Brightens
your leisure

Widens
your world

The STEELMARK on this tag tells you a product is made of steel.
Look for it when you buy.

The STEELMARK on this tag tells you a product is made of steel. Look for it when you buy.

AMBASSADOR BY RAMBLER

RAMBLER AMERICAN

BUICK

CHEVROLET

CHRYSLER

COMET

DODGE

OLDSMOBILE F-85

IMPERIAL

DODGE LANCER

LARK BY STUDEBAKER

PLYMOUTH

PONTIAC

RAMBLER CLASSIC

Steel is for going like '61

Here they are, the wonderful new '61's. They're fashioned in the most modern steels ... steels that take colorful finishes you'll be able to see yourself in years from now ... stainless steels that keep their sun-bright newness and clean up so easily you can laze through the job. Tough steel wheels soak up shock. Steel bumpers give you solid protection fore and aft. Steel bodies stay in shape, keep appearances up at trade-in time. You can count on steel in the new cars ... count on it for lasting beauty and value. Your dealer can show you—see him!

CADILLAC

CORVAIR

DODGE DART

DE SOTO

FALCON

FORD

STUDEBAKER HAWK

LINCOLN CONTINENTAL

MERCURY

OLDSMOBILE

BUICK SPECIAL

PONTIAC TEMPEST

VALIANT

USS United States Steel

1960

Felt tip pens, lasers and pacemakers were innovations of 1960. Fidel Castro tossed American companies out of Cuba, after the firms helped toss the Echo I communications satellite into orbit. Also in orbit were the democrats, who put John F. Kennedy in the White House in November.

Americans tuned their portable radios to hear such songs as "The Twist," "Itsy Bitsy Teenie Weenie Yellow Polka-Dot Bikini" and "Are You Lonesome Tonight?" Big movies included "Psycho," "Exodus," "Never on Sunday," "Butterfield Eight" and "The World of Susie Wong." Sheriff Taylor, Barney, Oppie and Aunt Bea visited millions of homes on television.

"Camelot," "Bye-Bye Birdie" and "The Unsinkable Molly Brown" were leading stage productions. Best selling books included *Born Free*, *To Kill a Mockingbird* and *The Rise and Fall of the Third Reich*.

Each month brought exciting headline stories: a new French currency in January, an atomic sub at the North Pole in February and major earthquakes and tidal waves in Morocco in March. Other 1960 events included: (April) first successful underwater launch of a Polaris missile; (May) American U-2 "spy" plane shot down over Soviet territory; (June) SS colonel Adolf Eichman snatched by Israeli agents from Argentina; (July) civil war breaks out in the Congo; (August) Olympic games open in Rome, Italy; (September) Hurricane Donna hits Atlantic Coast with 120 miles per hour winds; (October) Pittsburgh Pirates defeat New York Yankees in World Series; Yankee Skipper Casey Stengel fired; (November) Americans Willard Libby and Donald Glaser win Nobel prizes and John F. Kennedy elected president; (December) history's worst aviation disaster takes place over New York Harbor.

Actors Clark Gable and Ward Bond and Keystone Kops producer Mack Sennett passed away, along with songster Oscar Hammerstein II, philanthropist John D. Rockefeller and convict Caryl Chessman (whose execution sparked worldwide debate over capital punishment). Auto buffs also noted the deaths of Erwin "Cannonball" Baker, British four-wheel-drive pioneer Harry Ferguson, German automaker Karl Maybach and Delmar G. "Barney" Roos, father of the Jeep.

In sports, America's Floyd Patterson knocked out Sweden's Ingemar Johannson in a June title fight and the Minnesota Gophers were the top-ranked college football team. Pro football was just becoming a big-time sport, with Norm Van Brocklin, of the Philadelphia Eagles, foremost in the eye of fans. The American Football League (AFL) was brand new. The Boston Celtics won the National Basketball Association championship. In baseball, the Pittsburgh Pirates took the treasure at the World Series.

Civil rights demonstrations, spy trials, Britain's "Royal Family" (plus commoner Anthony Armstrong Jones), atom smashers, Japanese industry, Red China, the Irish Republican Army, Middle East frictions, disarmament agreements and film censorship were also big news makers.

As you can tell, things haven't changed very much in the past 33 years!

GO RAMBLER IN 1960
The New Standard of Basic Excellence

RAMBLER AMERICAN
2-DOOR SEDAN
$1795

AMERICA'S MOST EXPERIENCED BUILDER OF COMPACT CARS... Rambler Custom 4-Door Country Club Hardtop – Six or Rebel V-8.

A Rambler Custom four-door Country Club hardtop took this family on a kite-flying excursion near San Francisco's Golden Gate Bridge. The big news in bridges, during 1960, was the opening of the longest pre-stressed concrete span in the Western Hemisphere across Lake Oneida, near Brewerton, New York.

The 1960 U.S. Masters and U.S. Open were won by Arnold Palmer, a 30-year-old native of Ligonier, Pennsylvania. Fans who didn't have a new Ambassador Country Club hardtop to drive to the golf course could watch such tournaments on televisions, such as the Admiral Wide Angle 23-inch console model (inset).

Americans were starting to think small in 1960, when the nation's "Big 3" automakers brought out com-pacts. However, the small Metropolitan "1500" (on left), marketed by American Motors, had been around since 1954. Other products, such as Norelco's Speedshaver (on right), were growing smaller, too.

It seems the whole "Youngster's League" baseball team wants to try out the 1960 Rambler Custom Cross Country wagon purchased by one player's family. In Big League baseball, this was the year that the Pitts-burgh Pirates edged the New York Yankees in a seven-game World Series that ended on October 13.

In the 1960 art world, New York's Brooklyn Museum made news with a fabulous exhibit of Egyptian sculpture of the late period. The sculptured styling of the latest Buick Invicta station wagon also looked very artistic, especially when seen outside the Enos A. and Sarah DeWaters Art Center in Michigan.

We attended Brooklyn Technical High School in 1960, riding the ferry between Staten Island and Manhattan and a subway to Brooklyn. We never saw this Buick LeSabre, although the Statue of Liberty was a familiar sight. Yankee Skipper Casey Stengel (inset) was fired soon after he lost the World Series.

Buick also used a New York backdrop for this ad, showing "New York's Finest" admiring a LeSabre convertible. The license plate in the photo was altered to disguise which state it's from, but we're certain that's Central Park in the background. The population of New York City, in 1960, was 7,781,985 people.

Music fans rioted at the 1960 Newport Jazz Festival on 4th of July weekend. In England, a riot brought an end to a jazz festival held at the estate of Lord Montague (a famous name in motoring history) outside London. The "jazzy" Buick Invicta convertible was offered with a Delco radio that made sweet music.

THE TURBINE DRIVE BUICK '60

Divide and conquer
your space problem with walls
of Weldwood paneling

Michigan's Chuck Thompson became the first speed-boater to win the President's Cup four times with "Miss Detroit." An upscale family sought fun, rather than fame, with its Michigan-based boat. They hauled it with a new Buick LeSabre hardtop sedan. While the boat was probably fiberglass, Weldwood real wood paneling (inset photo) was the "in thing" for upscale American homes in 1960.

John F. Kennedy, of Massachusetts, defeated Richard M. Nixon in the closest-ever presidential race. This advertisement pictured a 1960 Cadillac Coupe DeVille in Nantucket, Massachusetts. The mother and daughter in another Cadillac advertisement (inset) had the popular "Jackie Kennedy look."

Cadillac Motor Division was the "gem" of General Motors and featured some of 1960's most fashionable jewelry in its advertising. In this case, we see the company's "V" and crest interpreted in sapphires and diamonds by Black, Starr & Gorham, Incorporated, a leading jewelry company of the day.

In 1960, dresses with matching jackets or coordinated coats were fashionable. Hats were more wearable, with off-the-face and halo brims. This mother and daughter ensemble was created for Cadillac, by the designer Scaasi. It wasn't in the S & H Green Stamps Ideabook, even though it promised "distinguished merchandise." Such trading stamp catalogs were popular with many average Americans during the 1960s.

A basset hound with the unusual name Champion The Ring's Banshee was one of America's top prize-winning dogs in 1960, capturing more group honors than any other hound. The perfect car for hauling beagle hounds to a meet was the 1960 Chevrolet Kingswood nine-passenger station wagon. Hey, where did that pesky cat come from?

Mikhail Tai of Riga, Latvia, took the 1960 world's chess championship from Mikhail Botvinnik, after a two-month, 24-game match in Moscow. These Chevrolet Bel Air Sport Coupe owners didn't play the game that seriously. The only "records" they were interested in were the type they could spin on their portable turntable.

It was a year of change for America. In Washington, a new president was heading for the White House. In Detroit, the innovative Corvair signaled a rethinking of the domestic automobile's size and technology. Women, like these Corvair fans, could also change the color of their hair, at home, with help from Miss Clairol (inset ad).

For the third time in a row, in 1960, Carlton Mitchell, of Annapolis, Maryland, took the Newport-to-Bermuda ocean race with his yawl Finisterre. Other boaters preferred sailing on calmer waters. Sailing into 1960 with virtually no changes from 1959 was the racy-looking Chevrolet Corvette.

"The Big Circus," a 1959 melodrama starring Victor Mature, Red Buttons and Rhonda Fleming, probably helped to inspire this advertisement claiming "you'll feel like a kid at the circus every time you take a spin in your new Chrysler." It also suggested that this 1960 New Yorker Sport Coupe was as strong as an elephant.

Remember when department stores catered to kids at Christmas? We'll never forget dad taking us to Macy's, in New York, in the 1960s. We'd see Santa, visit "Toyland" and marvel at the animated window displays. It was like a real "miracle on 34th Street." The 1960 Chrysler was also a marvel, with its push-button automatic transmission.

Venetian Way was the winner of the 86th Kentucky Derby. With Bill Hartack in the saddle, the Sunny Blue Farm's pony took a purse of $114,850. You didn't need quite that much money to purchase another winner built by Chrysler. The Imperial LeBaron four-door Southampton was, however, considered expensive, at $6,318.

In the fashion world, dress designer Ferdinando Sarmi and coat designer Jacques Tiffeau took two "Winnie" awards from the Coty American Fashion Critics. Another well-known designer, Nina Ricci, created the "Imperial Collection" to appear in this advertisement with the 1960 Chrysler Imperial Custom four-door Southampton.

The Scuba or aqualung was invented, in 1943, by Frenchmen Jacques-Yves Cousteau and Emil Gaghan. In the 1950s, recreational diving evolved. The new sport grew popular, with release of the television show "Sea Hunt," starring Lloyd Bridges. These divers went "beneath the surface" in examining the 1960 DeSoto's qualities.

In the early 1960s, about eight million Americans had boats and some 40,125,000 were boat hobbyists. Chris-Craft, Richardson and Wheeler were major makers of cabin cruisers (up to 35 feet) and motor yachts (35 feet and up), which cost up to $75,000. That's a lot more than the $3,663 price tag for the 1960 DeSoto Adventurer hardtop.

Some 50,000 square miles of scenic areas in the United States and Canada were set aside as National Parks, in 1960, and another 20,000 square miles as National Historic Parks. This family drove a Dodge Dart Pioneer station wagon to one of the 37 sites (29 National Parks and eight National Historic Parks) located in the United States.

Americans put in about a half hour less on the job in 1960 and production workers averaged a wage above $100 per week for the first time. Amusement parks boomed, as people found themselves with more money and leisure time. Dodge's Dart Phoenix four-door hardtop, with a slant six, was one way to save more money for family fun.

The International Air Transport Association reported that its members carried 106 million international and domestic passengers, topping the 100 million mark for the first time, in 1960. Orders for 900 new jets were placed that year. The big "D" in aircraft building was the Douglas DC-8, which traveled at a speed of 10 miles a minute.

The big "D" in automaking was the full-size Dodge Matador, shown here as a two-door hardtop. Ads said "dignity and imagination mark its distinctive design." With a big 383-cubic-inch V-8, Dodges could also travel fast. A special supercharged 1960 Dart, driven by Norm Thatcher, flew over the Bonneville Salt Flats at 191.8 miles per hour.

Decreased bag limits and hunting seasons, set by the Department of the Interior in 1959, continued in 1960. The shooting of canvasback and redhead ducks was prohibited, due to concerns over the plight of migratory waterfowl. No wonder these hunters had time to check out a 1960 Edsel Ranger that drove by their favorite spot.

The 1960 Edsels were introduced on October 15, 1959 and the marque was discontinued on November 19, 1959. Brought out with a great deal of hoopla, hyping it as "entirely new to the industry," the Edsel first bowed on September 4, 1957. It lasted just over three years. Only 76 of these 1960 Ranger convertibles were ever made.

Radio-controlled, gas-engined model airplanes appealed to many aviation buffs and model-building hobbyists during 1960. Every kid in America wanted to own one of these exciting and colorful toys. In the new-for-1960 compact car field, the model that everyone seemed to want to own was the Falcon. Ford sold 435,676 of them.

In the days before they became major television stars, Charley Brown, Lucy, Snoopy, Linus and Schroeder did a sales pitch for Ford's 1960 Fairlane 500 and Falcon. The Peanuts crew, created by Don Schulz for the United Features Syndicate, today remain among the most popular of all newspaper comic strip characters.

Alice's Adventures in Wonderland *was written in 1865 by Lewis Carroll. The kids' classic was turned into a Walt Disney animated film in 1951. Nine years later, Ford featured Alice and friends in an ad touting a pair of Falcons as "two new-size wonders." Kids also enjoyed Post Alpha-Bits (lower inset photo) in 1960.*

From 1950 to 1960, the number of children under 14 years of age increased by 15 million and came to represent 31 percent of America's population. While the growth rate flattened later, the numbers explain why 1960 ads for both Falcon station wagons and Colgate dental cream (with Gardol) had obvious appeal to kids and families.

Astronomers at Palomar Observatory identified and studied a new galaxy in 1960. It proved to be the most remote object known to science, six billion light years away. A 1960 Galaxie located no farther away than the local Ford dealer, was this beautiful Town Victoria. It could hold three "gridiron greats" (inset photo) on its chair-high seats.

There were 182.2 million people living in 52.6 million households in the United States in 1960. Sixty-four percent lived in urban households, even though eight of the 10 largest cities lost people for the first time ever in a national census. That still left plenty of customers in big cities for small businessmen using Ford F-100 pickup trucks.

For 1960, the Department of Defense provided $91,180,000 for United States Marine Corps procurements. It cost a lot less to procure a new Ford Thunderbird. The four-passenger sports/luxury hardtop had a base retail price of $3,755. The optional sliding sun roof was only $212 extra.

What a difference between the size of America's 1960 cars! According to Pictograph Corporation, a typical 1960 compact was 180 inches long, while the longest low-priced sedan was 210-9/10 inches. At 227.2 inches, the Lincoln Continental Mark V convertible beat them all. The dress shown in a Lincoln ad (inset) was fashionable in 1960.

The 1960 Lincoln Continental Mark V Landau Sedan was also a huge 227.2 inches long. That compared to average American car lengths (for popular, low-priced sedans) of 185-1/2 inches in 1936; 197-3/4 inches from 1942 to 1948; and 197-13/16 inches from 1949 to 1958.

The Brooklyn Bridge was 77 years old in 1960. Mercury used it to stress the "best built" slogan for its Monterey hardtop. The span linking Brooklyn and Manhattan was designed by John Roebling and completed by his son Washington. On the other side of New York City, the George Washington Bridge got a new lower deck in 1960.

1960 was the biggest year in United States construction history (inset), with $55 billion dollars spent. Private non-farm residential construction fell 10.3 percent, due to the growing popularity of multi-story dwellings. Apartment buildings with balconies were in style and provided a nice way to see the new Mercury Park Lane convertible.

A trend towards using plants as decorations in every room of American homes was evident in the early 1960s. The perfect car for hauling house plants was the 1960 Mercury Comet station wagon. Although compact-sized, it offered 76 cubic feet of storage space, which was as much as was provided in some standard size wagons.

FASHION

first of the compact cars with fine-car styling and priced with or below other compact cars

Clayton Ewing, of Green Bay, Wisconsin, sailed his yacht Dyna to Class A honors in the 1960 Newport-to-Bermuda ocean race. Two fashionable forms of Class A land transportation were the Comet station wagon and two-door sedan. In women's fashions, the furs and tall, top-heavy hats seen in a Mercury ad (inset) were in vogue.

The Federal-aid Act of 1960 authorized funds for future construction on the regular Federal-aid highway system and public domain roads totaling $2.09 billion. Total expenditures on highways, for 1960, were projected at $6.7 billion. That seemed like enough to keep this family's Oldsmobile "98" station wagon cruising smoothly along the highway.

Including performances at the Olympics in Rome, Italy, swimmers from the United States and Australia shattered 32 world records during 1960. The American aquatic champs included Mike Troy, George Harrison, Dick Blick, Jeff Farrell and Chris von Saltza. An automotive champ of the year was the Oldsmobile "98" two-door Sports Coupe.

Switzerland's 23-year-old skiing star Rogert Staub sped so quickly down KT-22 Mountain, at the 1960 Winter Olympics in Squaw Valley, California, that only four competitors came within two seconds of his time. A slower pace suited skiers arriving at Badger Pass, in Yosemite National Park, with an Oldsmobile "98" Holiday Sport Sedan.

The 1960 census put the population of South Dakota at 680,514. That did not include the buffalo that lived in Custer State Park. As you can see, the tourists in this family contributed to America's $2.3 billion photographic sales industry by purchasing lots of cameras. They also purchased a new Oldsmobile Dynamic "88" Fiesta three-seat station wagon.

Small Wonder —Valiant—the compact car with room, zoom, good looks to spare ... the car you'd want at *any* price! **Small Wonder,** Gothe's imported chiffon cotton in bloom ... a dress with a petit point wisp of jacket. ▼

Gothé

Another 1960 car ad focusing on fashion featured Chrysler's new Valiant compact wagon and a dress designed by Gothe. Shorter hemlines and briefer sleeves made dresses "compact," too. High, round "jewel" necklines were another trend in ladies' fashions. Short, sleek "cap" cuts were the hair styling hit of the year.

A 1960 Valiant leaves a production line at a modern Chrysler assembly plant. Factory sales of passenger cars rose 19 percent that year, to 6.74 million. Other motor news of 1960 included the obituaries of early race driver "Cannonball" Baker, pioneer German automaker Karl Maybach and "Barney" Roos, creator of the Jeep.

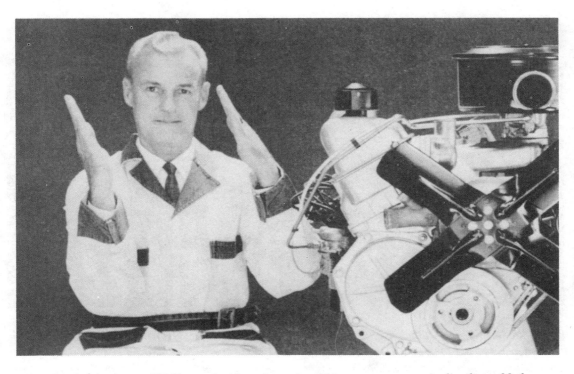

A Chrysler development of 1960 was the slant six engine. This new motor was inclined at a 30-degree angle, to allow space for an advanced manifold system that made important contributions to its performance and high economy. It gave 20 percent more passing power and used 15 percent less gas than other six-cylinder power plants.

After the Highway Trust Fund was overdrawn, a Congressional Investigation of the Highway Program began in 1960. The Congressional House Special Highway Investigating Subcommittee held hearings on irregularities in road building. The highway near a 1960 Plymouth Fury seems anything but regular, though it's impressive.

Tunnels in the news in 1960 included a subway tunnel in Toronto made by a new "cut then cover" technique, a new 44-mile-long tunnel opened through New York's Catskill Mountains and a $13 million car tunnel at the Lincoln Memorial in Washington, D.C. This 1960 Plymouth Fury sped through a tunnel to test its quietness.

Ships carried a record number of passengers across the Atlantic in 1960. Four new British liners, plus the 32,000-ton Leonardo da Vinci of the Italian line and the French Line's flagship, named France, were introduced. Television's "Gail Storm Show" (Oh, Suzannah!) featured an ocean liner and so did this Pontiac Bonneville Vista Sedan ad.

Seattle, Washington had 557,087 residents in 1960. Most were looking forward to the October 1, 1962 opening of the Seattle World's Fair. It was the first for America since the 1939-1940 World's Fair in New York City. This ad for Kelly Springfield tires showed a 1960 Pontiac Bonneville convertible by the 600-foot high Space Needle.

At the 1960 Winter Olympics in Squaw Valley, Germany's Helmut Recknagel made the longest jump of 306 feet. Although these recreational skiers couldn't sail that far, they were "jumping for joy" over the looks of the 1960 Pontiac Bonneville Sports Coupe. "Like the freshness of tingling, bracing mountain air," said the ad copy.

When the skiing was over, the Pontiac fans could visit their local A & P to have the man with the red bow tie whip up a pound of custom-ground coffee. Back then, most of the company's supermarkets sported look-alike colonial styling and all of the A & P stores had red A & P Coffee Service machines

In 1960, the United States had 20,953 miles of inland waterways linking lakes and other bodies of water, but the only way to get a 1960 Studebaker Lark VII two-door sedan across this lake was via this rather ancient ferry boat. The suggestion on the sign to "please set hand brake" seems like very good advice to us.

The Merricks were ready to go into business with a 1960 Studebaker Champ truck, America's lowest priced pickup. They probably put their phone number on the side so this woman (inset) could order their services with her kitchen extension wall phone. In October 1960, the Bell system tested a new experimental electronic switching system.

1961

John F. Kennedy (JFK) took the reins of power, in America, as 1961 dawned. In his farewell address, President Dwight D. Eisenhower warned Americans about the military industrial complex. The Pope warned Catholics about materialism and birth control. Chou En-lai warned Moscow that the romance was over.

Innovations of the year ranged from non-dairy creamer, to improved "measles shots," to the creation of an element called Lawrencium. An experimental voice recognition device held amazing promise for future generations. A wall erected between East and West Berlin held ominous possibilities. On the lighter side, New York Yankee baseball player Roger Maris hit a record 61 home runs.

The "Space Race" continued and the world was full of "hot spots." Fidel Castro turned up the heat in Cuba by taking a pro-Soviet, Marxist bent. Malcolm X steered his followers on a black power bent. In a small start to what would become a tidal wave of determination, a handful of pacifists made their way from San Francisco to Moscow on a peace march. But, as if to prove peace was an elusive goal, Cuban exiles launched the Bay of Pigs invasion. Some said JFK erred big by encouraging, but not backing the doomed effort.

The inauguration of JFK kicked off 1961 in January. On February 13, Patrice Lamumba was murdered in Katanga province, in the Congo. March marked the birth of the Peace Corps. Nazi Adolph Eichman went on trial, in Israel, for his World War II crimes, while Uri Gurgaran, a Russian cosmonaut, went into orbit. May brought attacks on civil rights-seeking "freedom riders" in Alabama and martial law in South Korea. South Africa became a republic. Kuwait gained its independence from Britain on June 19. A week later, Iraq claimed that Kuwait was a part of it.

A new crime called skyjacking originated on July 24, when a plane was diverted to Cuba by an armed passenger. In August, Russia said it was resuming nuclear bomb tests. An airplane crash killed United Nations General Secretary Dag Hammarskjold on September 18. In October, Soviet tanks were deployed in East Berlin. Russia, Britain and America turned down a "don't test bombs" plea from the United Nations on November 6. On December 27, Britain sent troops to the Persian Gulf when Iraq's premier Kassem hinted he was ready to "annex" Kuwait.

Americans were singing "Moon River," "Happy Birthday Sweet 16," "Hit the Road Jack," and (one of my favorites) "Big John."

New television series included "Hazel," "Dr. Kildare," "The Dick Van Dyke Show" and "Ben Casey" (another doctor show). In movie theaters, Americans saw "The Hustler," "A Raisin in the Sun," "The Absent Minded Professor," "West Side Story," "The Guns of Navarone" and "Breakfast at Tiffany's." Stage actors brought them "Come Blow Your Horn," "The Caretaker," "A Man for All Seasons," "The Night of the Iguana" and "How to Succeed in Business Without Really Trying." *The Agony and the Ecstasy*, *The Carpetbaggers*, and *The Making of the President, 1960* were among best-selling books.

Among the famous people dying were painter Grandma Moses, baseball legend Ty Cobb and Speaker of the House Sam Rayburn ("Mr. Sam" was almost always described this way, as if "Speaker of the House" was part of his given name). Hollywood lost Leo Carillo, who played Pancho in the "Cisco Kid," Gary Cooper, Chico Marx and Marion Jordon (who was Molly in "Fibber McGee and Molly"). Literary greats Ernest Hemingway, James Thurber and Dasheill Hammett passed from the scene.

Automotive personalities who departed included 74-year-old Powel Crosley, Jr. (on March 28) and 71-year-old Charles E. Wilson. President of General Motors from 1940 to 1953 and Secretary of Defense from 1953 to 1957, Wilson's death came September 26. On April 21, opera, as well as the car collecting hobby, lost singer James Melton.

Ambassador Adlai E. Stevenson was United States Representative to the United Nations in 1961. He dealt with a variety of "hot spots" from Cuba to the Congo. Another "ambassador" in the news that year was the Ambassador Custom four-door sedan built by American Motors.

How do you become an "American President" before you enter politics? George Romney did! He was president of American Motors. Then, he quit to run for governor of Michigan in 1962. During 1961, Romney brought out a new compact-size Rambler American convertible.

In 1961, botanists found that many plants suffered injury from exposure to ozone in concentrations less than one part per million in air, over periods as short as two hours. Such damage was increasingly seen around large cities. However, the plants behind this 1961 Buick Invicta two-door hardtop look quite healthy.

This building reflects International architecture, which was considered trendy in 1961. Flat surfaces and the use of glass as a structural material were characteristics of this style. This 1961 Buick LeSabre four-door hardtop also used lots of glass, though its sculptured body panels were anything but flat.

Dolls were among over $1.7 million worth of toys sold in 1961. In 10 years, the American toy industry's sales had doubled. Sales of Cadillacs, like the series Sixty-Two convertible, went up during the same period, but not by as big a percentage. They stood at 138,379 in 1961, versus 110,340 a decade earlier.

This San Francisco Opera House visitor, in a Cadillac ad (left), wore an opera gown and cape by Norman Norell. Another ad from the luxury car maker (right) featured a 1961 Fleetwood with French embroidery from the Boston Museum of Fine Arts and a jeweled "V" and crest by Black, Starr and Gorham.

One of more than 8 million boats plying American waters in 1961 was the Delta Queen. The restored paddle wheeler, sailing the Ohio River, appeared in the background of a Chevrolet Impala convertible publicity photo. On shore, women's bathing suits (inset) were predominantly, but not always, one-piece.

The tire and tire products branch of the rubber industry accounted for 39.3 percent of its total sales. About 25 percent of the market belonged to United States Rubber Company. This photo, from a 1961 tire advertisement, shows a picture of traffic conditions in 1961, when 76,007,000 American cars were registered.

Over two years, recreational fishing on United States federal land doubled to an estimated 1.88 million man-days. States and island possessions were given $5,485,000 in funds for sport fish restoration in 1961. This fisherman and woman got to their favorite fishing hole in a Chevrolet Impala Sport Coupe.

Lingering interest in America's frontier heritage was reflected in release of the 1961 film "The Alamo." Passion for the pioneers wasn't as strong as in the 1950s, though. The film started as a "special-attraction" and became a box office disappointment. Not disappointing was the 1961 Chevrolet Nomad wagon.

Though not a snowy year, 1961 saw a heavy snowstorm cover an area from the Central Great Plains to New England between December 22 and 25. Drifts in New York City were 10 feet high. The 1961 Corvair, with its rear-mounted, air-cooled engine, was a good car to operate in snow.

During 1961, the average use of electricity in the United States reached 4,810 kwh per citizen. A modern kitchen (right) featured 13 electric appliances from a knife sharpener to a television. The 1961 Corvair Lakewood station wagon fans on the right (not counting the dog) used nearly 15,000 kwh.

Camper-days in America's national parks topped the four million mark in 1961. One reason was most workers got three weeks of vacation, versus two in 1946. It was the 100th anniversary of organized camping in the United States, but many preferred their own campers, like the 1961 Corvair Greenbrier.

By 1961, one-fourth (11,250 miles) of the 41,000-mile National Interstate and Defense Highway System was open. The Federal Highway Act of 1961 increased Interstate System authorizations by $11.56 million. Some folks, like these Corvette lovers, still preferred driving the winding back roads.

In the United States, the 1961 Men's National Alpine Ski Championship was won by 18-year-old Rod Hebron of Canada. A great car to drive to the ski slopes was a Chrysler Newport four-door hardtop. Its "Firebolt" V-8 could burn regular gas, though it still couldn't sneak by many gas stations (inset photo).

A good way to check out the fashion trends of 1961 is to look at luxury car advertisements. This one, promoting the 1961 Chrysler Imperial Crown four-door Southampton finished in Alaskan White, shows a model in a dress designed by Roxanne, for Samuel Winston.

Unibody makes room for people, leaves no room for squeaks and rattles

1961 DE SOTO

"Unibody Construction" was said to add both space and quiet to the 1961 DeSoto two-door hardtop. Unfortunately, it added very little to the marque's sales. This was destined to be the last year that the nameplate was marketed. In fact, production was halted before the start of calendar-year 1961.

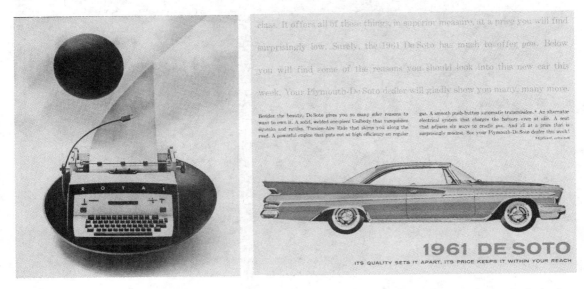

1961 DE SOTO

ITS QUALITY SETS IT APART, ITS PRICE KEEPS IT WITHIN YOUR REACH

Crisply-sculpted styling lines and an overall clean look were the keynotes of product design early in the 1960s. They can be seen in both the appearance of the 1961 Royal Electric Typewriter (left) and the 1961 DeSoto two-door hardtop (right). Chrysler continued its fins this year, but cut the use of chrome.

Lancer — The new compact by Dodge gives you a "bigger charge" out of the coldest winter driving.

The New Haven Railroad, which operated an important commuter rail line between New York City and Connecticut, became the first railroad to go broke since before World War II. This commuter, arriving home after dark, will appreciate the new alternator electrical system in his 1961 Plymouth Valiant.

America's piers were busy in 1961, as ocean-borne foreign trade (exclusive of trade with Canada) was nearly 20.2 million long tons per month. In addition, 1,469,351 passengers traveled out of the country on ships. The 1961 Dodge Dart convertible was a great way to get to the point of departure.

Railway Age magazine called 1961 "disastrous" for railroad finances. The Interstate Commerce Commission proposed that federal subsidies be paid to maintain "essential" railroad passenger services. An essential item for many rail commuters was a 1961 Dodge Dart station wagon waiting at the station.

American families got around in various ways in 1961. United Airlines (above, left) offered the world's largest jet fleet for the convenience of long-distance travelers. Those sticking closer to home, could appreciate the roomy comfort of the full-size Dodge Custom 880 station wagon (above, right).

Hurricane Carla hit in September, 1961, causing 46 deaths, 500 injuries and $200 million in damages. East Texas got 10 to 16 inches of rain. Of course, it was nice and dry inside this 1961 Thunderbird hardtop. The umbrella-toting gal could dry her hair quickly with her Westinghouse hair dryer (inset photo).

At the 1961 Washington International Horse Show, the U.S. Equestrian Team won rider and horse trophies. Frank Chapot, of Wallpack, New Jersey took top rider honors with a thoroughbred named San Lucas. Another thoroughbred seen that year was the 1961 Ford Galaxie Starliner hardtop.

Trucking was a growth industry. Trucks hauled some 22 percent of the nation's inter-city freight, up from nine percent in 1946. During the same years, freight shipped by rail dropped from 67 percent to 45 percent. Ford's 1961 heavy truck line included tilt cab (left) and conventional (right) models.

Ford's 1961 Falcon Ranchero pickup was well-suited for those light landscaping jobs that home owners tackled on weekends.

Many young ladies tried out for cheer leading squads in 1961 (see below). Boys often went in for Cub Scouting.

In 1961, elementary school enrollments in the United States came to 34.2 million. Another 10.8 million students were enrolled in high schools. For many young women, becoming a member of a cheer leading squad was the highlight of high school. The 1961 Falcon Club Coupe also drew many cheers.

The Department of Commerce said that new construction hit $57.33 million for 1961, a three percent increase over the previous year. This gang of hard-hatted construction workers got to the job site in a 1961 International Harvester pickup with optional Travelcab.

Fort Wayne, Indiana's population was 161,776 in 1961. Among the best-known products made there were International Harvester trucks and tractors. Here we see a deluxe V-8 version of the 1961 International Harvester Travelall station wagon. Matthew E. Welsh was governor of the "Hoosier State" that year.

In 1961, over 67 percent of United States citizens, some 85,166,281 people, were married. They lived in about 53,291,000 households. A new citizen was born every 10.5 seconds. No wonder station wagons, even this Jeep model with styling that hadn't changed since 1946, were growing in popularity.

The year 1961 was the Jeep's 20th birthday. The first production Jeeps had been built for military use in World War II. This 1961 Universal CJ-5 is one of 15,269 such models manufactured that year. At this time, the Jeep and the International Scout were the leading four-wheel-drive recreational vehicles.

A 3,571-mile sailboat race, from Los Angeles to Tahiti, was held during 1961. The 63-foot yawl Athene, captained by San Francisco's James O. Willhite, won the handicap event. Another winner was the 1961 Lincoln Continental, with its industry-first 24,000-mile "pledge of excellence" warranty.

A 1961 Lincoln Continental on a romantic mountain top doesn't compare with the Himalayas. However, it reminds us that Nuptse, a 25,850-foot neighbor of Mount Everest, was ascended for the first time ever that year. The inset shows a Persian lamb coat lover who could warm even a mountain climber.

This advertising illustration shows the 1961 Mercury Comet four-door sedan near a group of rodeo cowboys. Actor Gary Cooper, star of many cowboy movies, passed away on May 13, 1961. Born on May 7, 1901, in Helena, Montana, Cooper won an Oscar for his role in the 1953 Western "High Noon."

In Oregon, the new Winema National Forest was established in 1961. It increased land administered by the United States Forest Service to 186.1 million acres. Recreational visits to National Forests climbed to over 100 million, a 12 percent increase. These visitors arrived in a new Mercury Meteor.

The roomy 1961 Oldsmobile 98 Holiday Coupe was a great way to get to an airport. America had 55 scheduled airlines with 1,900 aircraft and a half-million miles of routes. On July 24, a plane with 38 passengers was seized by an armed man and forced to fly to Havana, Cuba in the world's first skyjacking.

On May 5, 1961, Commander Alan Shepard was the first U.S. astronaut to take a sub-orbital flight at Cape Canaveral, Florida. On July 21, Virgil Grissom went 303 miles in 16 seconds inside a second space capsule launched in Florida. The 1961 Oldsmobile Starfire did not fly by those Florida palms quite that fast.

Billy Kidd won the 1961 Eastern Slalom Championship at Stowe, Vermont and took first place in the slalom runs at the Harriman Cup Ski Races in Sun Valley, Idaho. Like a championship skier, this 1961 Oldsmobile Super 88 Holiday Coupe could take on the steepest hills with its "Skyrocket" V-8 engine.

Some 123,000 firemen took training in municipal, state and Canadian Provincial programs in 1961. The
firemen of Engine Company 85 trained their eyes on a hot V-8-powered Oldsmobile F-85. Another hot
product of 1961 (inset) was the General Electric Toast-R-Oven. Hey, don't burn that muffin!

75

The last full year the U.S. Navy flew blimps was 1961. Some 150 had been used in World War II, including the Goodyear blimp "Mayflower." The Goodyear fleet was revived after the war. The Mayflower, alone, lasted past 1959. Its appearance in a 1961 Valiant ad recalls Plymouth's old Mayflower logo.

NEW PLYMOUTH WAGONS...
MIGHTY BIG ABOUT THEIR BEAUTY

(Just the opposite about their price)

The postwar "baby boom" filled station wagons, like this 1961 Plymouth, with kids. Some 48.7 percent of the United States population consisted of youngsters between five- and 19-years-old. That compared to 35.1 percent in 1950. Plymouth's ad promised "95 cubic feet of kid-and-cargo room."

In 1961, interest in radio-controlled model airplanes grew with the development of quieter motors. The Wen-Mac "Dauntless" dive bomber (inset) was made by AMF. The new motors reversed a decline in the hobby. The National Model Aeroplane Championships drew a record crowd. Not setting any sales records was the radically-styled 1961 Plymouth Fury.

American Machine and Foundry Corporation, better known as AMF, sold Voit brand aqualungs and skis (inset photo), as well as masks, fins and snorkels. You could probably fill the huge trunk of this 1961 Plymouth two-door hardtop with such water sports equipment, if you were driving to the beach.

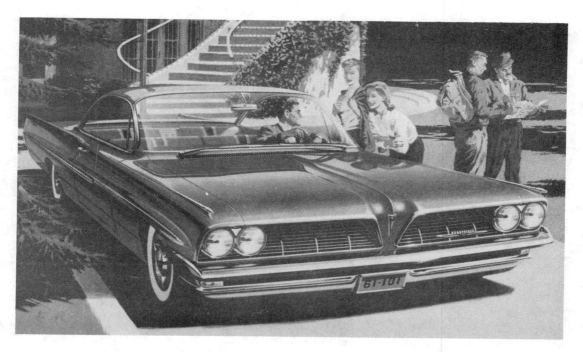

Several of the world's greatest peaks were ascended for the first time in 1961. In March, a party of climbers from America, England and New Zealand scaled the 22,494-foot summit of Ama Dablam. Climbing to new heights in the world of automotive styling was the 1961 Pontiac Bonneville Sports Coupe.

Hawaiians surfed long ago. The sport was banned by missionaries in 1821. Olympic swimmer Duke Kahanamoku revived it, forming the first surfing club in 1920. Light balsa, plastic and fiberglass boards of the mid-'50s led to a '60s surfing craze. The 1961 Pontiac Bonneville appealed to many young surfers.

About 33.4 million people flew domestic airlines in 1961. Few realized that planes of the future would have phone service, due to a microwave satellite communications system pioneered by Bell Telephone in 1961 (inset). Pontiac pioneered Wide-Track Drive in 1959 and featured it on all 1961 Bonnevilles.

On Christmas Day, 1961, Pope John XXIII revealed that the Roman Catholic Church would hold its 21st ecumenical council, at the Vatican, during 1962. In the United States, people kept busy shopping for Christmas trees or Pontiacs like the Safari station wagon (left) and the Tempest four-door sedan (right).

Judging by the license plates on the 1961 Studebaker Lark hardtop, this family added three people to the 16,782,304 population of New York. Nelson A. Rockefeller was governor of the Empire State that year. Among laws passed there, in 1961, was a measure banning billboards along Interstate Highways.

In July, 1961, President Kennedy asked congress for a comprehensive policy to aid development of national water resources. Public Law 87-88 promoting water treatment plants was passed. If this 1961 Studebaker Lark owner gets too much sun through her sun roof, she may need (inset) Revlon's "Contempera" make-up.

Imported car sales tapered off to about 300,000 units in 1961, as American manufacturers now offered a wide range of compact, mid-size and full-size models. About 60 European models were still sold here, however. One was the 1961 Triumph Herald Sports Coupe. It listed for $2,149.

While other foreign automakers saw their sales decline, Volkswagen continued to grow. In the first three quarters of 1961, Volkswagen was outselling six domestic compacts and six of 12 larger cars. This Volkswagen advertising photograph highlighted the reputation for good service that the company's dealership enjoyed in the early 1960s.

1962

Threats of war in Cuba, Laos, Vietnam, the Congo and along the Indian border kept politicians and reporters busy in 1962. The world said "Good-by Norma Jean" (to Marilyn Monroe) and "adios" to Richard Nixon, who "quit" politics, but not for long enough. On February 24, 1962, casino owner William F. Harrah opened his Harrah's Automobile Collection in Sparks, Nevada, a suburb of Reno.

"Freedom riders" continued their fights for civil rights and James Meredith, a Negro, was enrolled at the University of Mississippi. John F. Kennedy (JFK) opened the Seattle World's Fair by remote-control and French actor Yves Montaund came to American television via the Telestar satellite.

In January, JFK presented a budget, his first, with expenses of $92.5 billion and income of $93 billion. February sent "advisers" to Vietnam and America's first astronaut, John Glenn, into orbit. In March, Glenn got New York's biggest ever ticker tape parade, complete with 1954 Chrysler parade phaeton. A resumption of American nuclear testing was threatened that month, too. In April, the Ranger IV spacecraft crashed into the far side of the moon. The half-year ended with a Soviet spy escaping from New York to Israel, where he was jailed.

July brought a British cabinet shake up. In August, the Soviets launched two manned spacecraft and America sent a space probe sailing past Venus. Sonny Liston took the heavyweight boxing championship in September. JFK mobilized the National Guard to get James Meredith into "Old Miss." The New York Yankees won the World Series in October. A week later, America blockaded Cuba. The blockade ended in November, the same month the United States resumed atmospheric nuclear testing in the Pacific. In Cuba, 1,113 prisoner's from 1961's ill-fated Bay of Pigs invasion were released in exchange for $53 million in food, drugs and medicine.

Songs of the year included "Roses are Red," "Blowin' in the Wind," "The Wah-Watusi," "Mashed Potato Time," "Twistin' the Night Away," and "He's a Rebel." Virginia Woolf and Seidman and Son were on the stage. Films included "Birdman of Alcatraz," "Lawrence of Arabia," "Lolita" and "What Ever Happened to Baby Jane?" The "boob-tube" introduced us to the original "Beverly Hillbillies" and "The Lucy Show." Johnny Carson was a rookie on the "Tonight" show, replacing Jack Parr. New were 90-minute ("The Virginian") and 120-minute ("Combat") television shows. "Dr. Kildare" and "Ben Casey" were back for their second year.

Ken Kesey's *One Flew Over the Cuckoo's Nest*, James Baldwin's *Another Country*, and Jack Kerouac's *Big Sur*, were best-selling books.

Customized model car kits were a fast-growing trend. "The First Family," a Vaughn Meader comedy album, poked good natured fun at Jackie and JFK. In the art world, *Mona Lisa* visited America.

Who died in 1962? Nazi Adolph Eichman, novelist William Faulkner, cowboy movie star "Hoot" Gibson, comedian Ernie Kovacs, builder Arthur Levitt (creator of Levittown), gangster "Lucy" Luciano and former first lady Eleanor Roosevelt. Car personalities passing on included ex-General Motors president Curtice Harlow on November 3 and Packard V-12 designer Jesse Vincent.

The "beach bum" life was in during the 1960s and **Beachcomber** magazine came out. By 1962, dune buggies appeared on the West Coast. Early examples were little more than car chassis fitted with fat tires for fun driving on sand. Rambler's 1962 Ambassador V-8 station wagon was also a "fun driving" car.

Maceo Pincard, a songwriter whose tune "Sweet Georgia Brown" was popular with Dixieland bands, passed away in New York City on July 19, 1962. This three-piece Dixieland band provided the entertainment at a lawn party that attracted several Ramblers, including a new 1962 American convertible.

Trends in men's wear, for 1962, included hats with triangular convex crowns, two-button suits (as preferred by President John F. Kennedy) and plaid sport coats. Also fashionable was the 1962 Buick LeSabre four-door hardtop in shiny black with narrow white sidewall tires.

Richly textured silk and brocade ball gowns (inset) were usually of full-length design in 1962. One-piece swimsuits were the best sellers, but two-piece suits were gaining and, soon, designer Rudi Gernreich's daring topless bathing suit would appear. This topless 1962 Buick Invicta convertible had a Wildcat 455 V-8.

Skirts and dresses with crisp, swinging shapes made fashion news in 1962. They came in pleated, umbrella-tucked, flared or "matchbox" styles. The latter was designed by Dior's fashion house. Cadillac's 1962 Series 62 convertible also had a crisp and fashionable look, with its heavy body sculpturing.

About $79 million worth of life insurance was sold in 1962, bringing the value of all policies owned by Americans to a record $725 million. Pay-outs hit $9.3 billion. The owner of this chauffeur-driven 1962 Cadillac Fleetwood limousine might be picking up a check at this Michigan Life Insurance Company office.

There was a revival of interest in women's furs, in 1962, due to First Lady "Jackie" Kennedy's influence. Pointed shoes (inset photo), with an Italian flair, were popular for men that season. These Jarman Astro Jets cost $10.95 to $19.95. The 1962 Cadillac Coupe de Ville still had pointed fins.

This upper income couple probably helped the Internal Revenue Service celebrate its 100th birthday by sending in a fat tax payment. Abraham Lincoln established the "IRS," to help with post-Civil War reconstruction, through a law signed on July 1, 1862. Another fat check could buy that Cadillac Sedan de Ville.

The United States Coast Guard was charged with promoting boating safety and law enforcement in peacetime. It rendered 35,848 assistance calls to boaters during 1962 and saved 2,597 lives from peril. The 1962 Chevrolet Impala SS Sport Coupe helped save Chevrolet's performance car reputation.

According to John D. Green, president of the American Hotel and Motel Association, over $1 billion was spent, in 1962, to build new hotels and motels and refurbish old ones. Today, car collectors are investing lots of money, each year, to refurbish thousands of 1960s vehicles like this Chevrolet Impala sedan.

The United States Department of Health, Education and Welfare reported that the national birth rate in 1962 was 22.5 live births for every 1,000 citizens, a 3.2 percent decline from the same period in 1961. For growing families, the 1962 Chevrolet Nova 400 station wagon was an excellent car.

Even this small country school was affected by the debate, over prayers and Bible readings in public schools, that shook America in 1962. Other news included Bell's System's School-to-Home Telephone Service (inset), to teach shut-ins. Car buyers learned about Chevrolet's economical new Chevy II Nova.

The 175th anniversary of the Indian Botanical Garden, probably the largest in Asia, was celebrated on July 6, 1962. On a much smaller scale, this florist grew plants and flowers to sell from his roadside cart. They attracted the attention of a pair of 1962 Corvair Monza Coupe owners, who stopped to make a purchase.

Florida was a great place to cruise in a 1962 Corvette convertible. To stay slim while vacationing there, drinking Borden's ready (inset) was a good idea. The state's population grew as Cuban refugees flocked to Miami and a military build-up began when president Kennedy imposed his Cuban blockade on October 22.

At New York's Roosevelt Raceway, Irvin Paul won the 1962 National Pacing Derby with the fastest 1-1/4-mile trotting contest ever. His time was two minutes and 29.6 seconds. A car that set the pace was Chrysler's 1962 Newport four-door sedan. Full-sized, and featuring a 265-horsepower V-8, it cost just $2,964.

Jack Nicklaus, a 22-year-old rookie golfer, took the 62nd United States Open Championship with a 71-stroke play-off round, against veteran Arnold Palmer's 74. Two other frequent visitors to golf courses were the 1962 Chrysler Sport 300 convertible and (inset photo) comedian and actor Bob Hope.

Americans into boating cheered when the Weatherly, a United States craft, defeated the Australian sloop Gretel, to retain the America's Cup. The race took place at Newport, Rhode Island in September. By that time, automakers were offering close-out sales on 1962 Dodge Dart 440 hardtops like this one.

The International Oceanographic Commission of the United States Educational, Scientific and Cultural Organization, held its second session, at Paris, France, in September 1962. Attracting an ocean of admirers was the new-for-1962 Dodge Lancer GT two-door hardtop.

During 1962, the United States Congress enacted legislation authorizing two new National Seashores at Padre Island, Texas and Point Reyes, California. This 1962 Dodge Dart 440 was a reliable car for outdoor lovers (inset photo) to take to the shore, for a 1960s-style beach party, on a cool summer night.

There were more than three million farmers in America in 1962. Many a farm boy put the money he made, for working from dawn to dusk, into a MoPar muscle car. When the milking, plowing and chores were done, that "big-block" '62 Dart 440 would come rumbling out of the barn to run the dark back roads.

"Who's Afraid of Virginia Woolf?" and "A Funny Thing Happened on the Way to the Forum," were two of 1962's notable stage productions. These Village Playhouse actors may not have seen Broadway, but they still enjoyed their hobby and their 1962 Ford Falcon Squire station wagon.

The guitar-strumming beach boy might be belting out "The Girl from Ipanema," "Blowin' in the Wind," "He's a Rebel" or "I Can't Stop Loving You." Do you think the latter was written by a 1962 Fairlane 500 owner about his car? Most likely, an RCA hi-fi (inset) was a better bet for anyone seeking to hear good music.

In auto racing, Rodger Ward took the Indy 500 and the winners of LeMans were Phil Hill, of the United States, and Oliver Gendering, of Belgium. England's Graham Hill took the International Trophy Race. Ford was promoting "Total Performance" and advertised the 1962 Galaxie 500/XL at a sports car race.

Cornell beat Yale 14 to 5 to win the National Intercollegiate Polo Championship for the second year in a row. Cornell's Frank Butler made seven goals and earned outstanding player honors. An outstanding car of the year was the 1962 Ford Galaxie 500/XL convertible with the optional 406-cubic-inch V-8.

Parachuting competitions began in 1936 in America. New equipment and techniques made skydiving (jumping from aircraft with a steerable parachute) popular in 1962. Later in the 1960s, paratroopers played a role in the Vietnam war. The 1962 Thunderbird Sport Roadster had an aircraft-inspired look.

RCA Service Company used 100 Ford Econolines on factory service calls for home televisions and appliances in 1962. RCA technicians were on call from 157 branch offices. The ad didn't say what kind of trucks the other 57 branches used. There were 608 television stations broadcasting in America that year.

During 1962, President John F. Kennedy established a new Bureau of Outdoor Recreation, in the Department of the Interior, to coordinate federal recreation programs and assist in developing similar state programs. The outdoor buffs shown here installed a camper body on their 1962 Ford Styleside Pickup.

The construction of new, non-farm homes, swung upwards in 1962. More than 1.4 million units were built in the United States. The GMC Suburban was a great vehicle for new homeowners. It could be used as a passenger and cargo-carrying station wagon (insert photo) or as a hard-working, light-duty truck.

Light-duty trucks continued to look fancier and more "automobile-like" during the early 1960s. The 1962 GMC Wide-Side pickup may be on this estate to help with gardening and landscaping chores, but an attractive two-tone paint scheme goes a long ways towards disguising its utilitarian nature.

Enrollment in all American schools, kindergarten through college, totaled 51.4 million in 1962. This included some 35 million in elementary grades; 11.7 million in high schools and 4.7 million in colleges. This 1962 International Travelall station wagon is depicted outside Lincoln Public School.

On December 8, 1962, scores of motorists were trapped when a severe snowstorm caused a 150-mile stretch of the Pennsylvania Turnpike to be closed to traffic. A little bit of snow ... or even a lot of snow ... had very little effect on the four-wheel-drive International Scout. It's shown here with an optional Travel-top.

At the end of 1962, there were 84,121 general aviation aircraft in the United States, plus 2,166 airline aircraft like this Delta Air Lines jet. This Midwest airline flew Douglas DC-8s and Convair 880s to Florida. Waiting to greet passengers at Tampa Airport was a 1962 Willys Jeep with the fringed-top Gala trim package.

Station wagons were in vogue in 1962. Kaiser Motor's Willys Jeep subsidiary continued to make wagons with styling very similar to early postwar models. However, the "guided missile" side trim moldings hinted of this vehicle's later vintage. It was available in two- and four-wheel-drive models.

President Kennedy's Accelerated Public Works Program, passed in October 1962, allocated $15 million for improvements to 83 National Forests in 34 states and Puerto Rico. This couple enjoyed the sights and sounds of a sunny day, while visiting a forest in their 1962 Lincoln Continental.

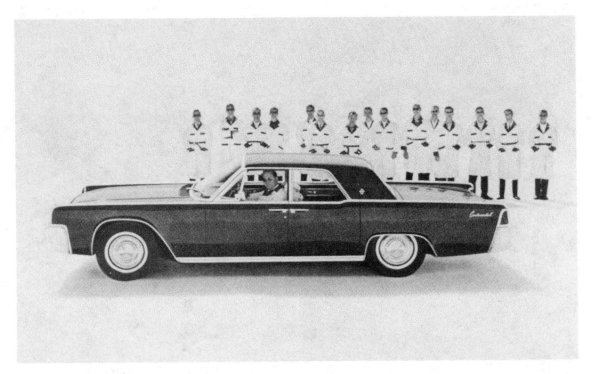

Maximillian Schell was voted best actor of 1962 for his moving performance in "Judgment at Nuremburg." These 16 test drivers had to pass judgment on every new Lincoln Continental that left the factory that year. "They tolerate nothing short of the highest standards," said Ford in this advertisement.

United States President John F. Kennedy (inset photo) had several special Lincoln Continentals at his disposal through the White House motor pool. Polls that year showed that "JFK's" mid-term popularity was the highest accorded to any president since the Franklin D. Roosevelt administration of the 1930s.

Ford built the "X-100" presidential car in early 1961. Removable sections permitted a variety of roof configurations for various functions. During 1962, this car returned to the factory for touch-up. A new 1962-style grille and bumper were added, then. The so-called "Kennedy" Lincoln is now in The Henry Ford Museum.

A record of nearly $12 billion was spent on national and local advertising, in the United States, during 1962. J. Walter Thompson Agency, which handled the Mercury account, retained its role as the largest agency with $40 million in billings. This photographer is busy making a 1962 Mercury advertisement.

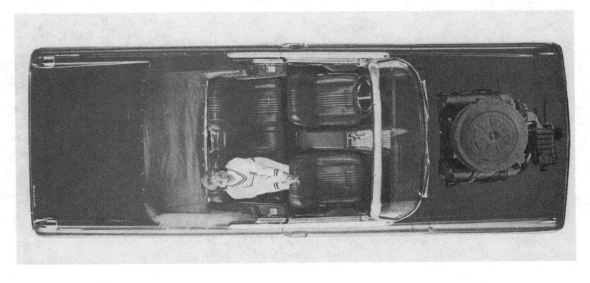

The bucket-seated 1962 Mercury Monterey S-55 convertible was photographed from above in one creative advertisement printed in magazines that year. American marketers spent $86.5 million on magazine advertising, versus $1.5 billion invested in television commercials.

Some 4.2-million metric tons of chromite, the ore used to make chromium, were produced in 1962. Mercury did its best to use as much as possible on the year's Monterey S-55 front end. The Sessions Clock Company also used lots of bright metal to highlight the glittery designs of its 1962 line of electric clocks.

United States swimmers dominated all comers at the outdoor swimming championships, in Japan, during 1962. They took 19 of 25 class titles and first place honors in 11 of 13 events. Many Americans now had a swimming pool at their home and a Mercury Monterey hardtop in the driveway.

Interest in balsa-wood model plane kits picked up during 1962, reversing a trend of several years. Most were flown in a circle, around an operator controlling them via a wire, but some were radio-controlled. The 1962 Oldsmobile F-85 Cutlass had aviation type features, such as bucket seats and a front console.

Southern California beat Notre Dame 25 to 0 to win 10 games in its first unbeaten season in 30 years. It then went on to whip Wisconsin in the Rose Bowl Game on New Year's Day. The 1962 Oldsmobile F-85 Cutlass could whip most American compacts with its 185-horsepower aluminum-block V-8.

Several bridges opened in 1962, including the Biloxi Bay Bridge in Mississippi and the Alexander Hamilton Bridge in New York. The first long delta girder bridge in the United States, was also completed, near Yakima, Washington. Bridging the gap between plain and fancy was a neat new 1962 Oldsmobile Dynamic 88.

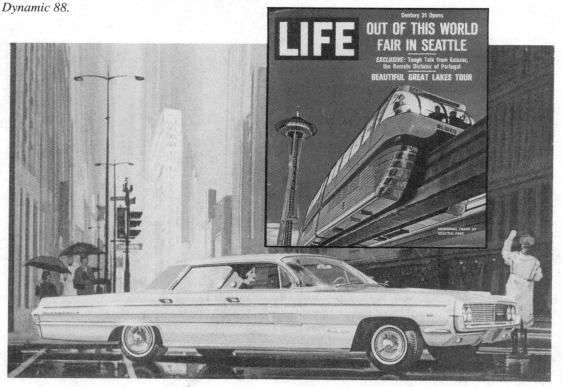

Seattle, Washington had an estimated population of 181,608 people in 1962. The Seattle World's Fair (inset), which opened there in the spring of 1962, was successful enough to attract 9,639, 969 paid admissions in its first season. The classy 1962 Oldsmobile Holiday Sports Sedan made its owner look successful.

These Sunday afternoon boaters were rowing for exercise and relaxation. In 1962's intercollegiate rowing competitions, Yale won the Blackwell Cup, Cornell won the Carnegie Cup and MIT won the Compton Cup. Meanwhile, the 1962 Plymouth Valiant won a medal, for good design, from the Society of Illustrators.

Easter Sunday fell on April 22 in 1962. These dressed-up young ladies may be heading for the Easter Parade in the family car. It's the 1962 edition of Plymouth's compact-size Valiant. Mom and dad could use a Kodak Starmite camera (inset photo) to take a snapshot for the family album. It was a compact, too.

The National Soaring Museum is at Elmira, New York and a national glider meet is held there each summer. Hot air balloons are the oldest form of flying and gliders are the oldest type of airplane. In the early 1960s, ballooning was revived as an aerial sport. A sporty 1962 car was the Plymouth Sport Fury convertible.

The 1962 Plymouth offered eight percent better gas mileage than the 1961 model, which took honors for class 6 in the Mobilgas Economy Run. Shown here is the Fury four-door sedan.

Pontiac introduced a new model called the Grand Prix in 1962. It took up where the Ventura left off, combining the Catalina-size body with more luxurious trim and a sports interior, plus the four-barrel carburetor of the Bonneville V-8. The "GP" was often depicted in European settings.

Call it the Tempest LeMans! (Luh-mahnz)

This is probably one of the poorest thought out car advertisements of the 1960s, since it advises readers to pronounce the name of Pontiac's 1962 Tempest "LeMans" differently than it would be said by a Frenchman. "Lay-ma" would be more correct. "Luh-mahnz" is an Americanized pronunciation.

Methods of making new types of human foods from fish protein concentrate (FPC) were examined by the Fish and Wildlife Service during 1962. A wide range of products, derived from dehydrated or de-fatted fish, was envisioned. These fishermen had room for all their gear in a 1962 Catalina Safari wagon.

Major Piero D'Inzeo earned 36 points to win the individual jumping title at the 1962 National Horse Show. The United States won the team championship with 104 points. Pontiac's 1962 Bonneville Sport Coupe was a winner in the new-car derby, with features, styling and performance that made good "horse sense."

Architecture was characterized by growing use of concrete. Buildings made of raw concrete were seen in tropical areas, while concrete and brick or concrete and glass, were common elsewhere. Studebaker's basic 1962 "architecture" hadn't changed in years, but it looked great on the Lark (left) and GT Hawk (right).

Champion Elfinbrook Simon, a white terrier, took top honors at the 86th Westminster Kennel Club dog show in 1962. A Pembroke Welsh corgi named Willet's Red Jacket took best in show at the National Capital Kennel Club event. The 1962 Studebaker Lark Daytona hardtop also had a winning pedigree.

1963

The assassination of president John F. Kennedy on November 22, 1963 immediately ended the celebration of the signing of a partial nuclear test ban. Kennedy's brutal and untimely death would stamp the rest of the '60s with a sense of lingering frustration. Only the wailing of four mop-topped Englishmen, known as the *Beatles*, seemed to alleviate the pain. Their first albumn was released in America in December, 1963.

Other tragedies marked the year: an earthquake in Yugoslavia, a hurricane in Haiti, flooding in Italy and the shooting of Medgar Evers in Jackson, Mississippi. Joe Valachi spilled the beans on his underworld cronies, Martin Luther King, Jr. led an inspired march on Washington and an American became a saint for the first time.

Month by month highlights began when Russia and the United States signed off on the Cuban crisis in January. There was no crisis, they said. In February, America gave official recognition to Iraq's Ba'athist government and underground A-bomb tests resumed in Nevada. In March, Chung Lee Park forgot his promises to hold South Korean elections. A new atomic submarine, the *Thresher*, sunk in April, killing its entire crew. On May 12, JFK sent troops to Birmingham, Alabama to quell racial unrest. Pope John XXIII died on June 3 and, on the 19th, the first woman (a Russian cosmonaut) rocketed into space. Kennedy made his famous "Ich bin ein Berliner" speech on the 26th and, two days later, Khrushchev was in Berlin, too.

A new pope, Paul VI, met JFK in July. In August, martial law hit South Vietnam, the Soviet-American "hot line" bowed and 200,000 civil rights marchers converged peacefully on Washington, D.C. In September, China and Russia squabbled and America signed the partial nuclear test ban. Britain's new prime minister, Alec Douglas-Home, took office on October 18. In November, fatal shots rung out from a Dallas, Texas book depository, smashing the life out of our nation's youthful leader. Lyndon Baines Johnson became president and America mourned. December found Greeks and Turks going at it in Cyprus. The year ended, but it was really just the beginning.

Sports news in 1963 summed up as Dodgers beat Yanks in World Series; Liston beats Patterson in the ring; Parnelli Jones beats the pack at Indy; and the Giants beat everyone in pro football. Rogers Hornsby, the baseball pioneer, died on January 7.

Top tunes of the year involved "Wives and Lovers," a "magic dragon" and "Muddah and Fadduh." "Cleopatra," "Tom Jones," and "Hud," packed them in at the movies. New to television viewers were the "Fugitive" and "Petticoat Junction." Actors Charles Laughton, ZaSu Pitts, Dick Powell and Jason Robard had their obituaries written.

On television, "My Favorite Martian" and the original "Fugitive" were hits of the new season. "Petticoat Junction" also bowed. On the stage, "Oliver" was "Barefoot in the Park," when it reached "110 in the Shade." *The Group, The Centaur* and *The American Way of Dying*, were tops in reading. Poet Robert Frost died.

Innovations included Polaroid film, the artificial heart and a legal lottery (in New Hampshire). An unsung auto parts inventor died. Ivar W. Brogger, who came to America from Norway, was credited with the first turn indicator.

It was a classic case of extra underdog effort, when two American skiers placed second and fourth at Norway's Hollmenkollen Ski Festival. Another classic of 1963 was the American Motors Rambler Classic 770 four-door sedan.

The 57-foot aluminum racing yacht Ondine won a 2,864-mile race from Newport, Rhode Island to Plymouth, England. Another sailing event of the year was the voyage of the Nina II (inset), a replica of Christopher Columbus' vessel of 1492. This sea captain set sail in a 1963 Rambler American 440 convertible.

This fellow may be relaxing his arm after winding his way through MGM's original cast recording from the musical "She Loves Me." The longer, two-record album broke new ground. Earlier double albums all recorded live concerts or historical collections. The 1963 Buick Special sedan was also a longer car.

The closer you get to Riviera, the further it is from everything else on the road.

Women's fashion trends of 1963 included a preference for patterned cloths, especially with large hound-stooth checks, giant Glen plaids and various stripes. "Mannish" looking hats were also in vogue. The lady seems to be very stylishly attired and her 1963 Buick Riviera's up-to-date design fits right in.

In 1963, horse racing's Triple Crown for three-year-olds was split between Chateaugy and Candy Spots. The former pony took the Kentucky Derby and the Belmont Stakes, but Candy Spots saw victory in the Preakness. A winner in the ragtop popularity race was the 1963 Buick Skylark convertible.

American consumers regained confidence in the economy and retail sales jumped six percent to $245 billion per year. Increases were noted in many categories, with apparel sales up two percent and home finishings up five percent. The 1963 Buick LeSabre Coupe was another frequently purchased commodity.

Not counting sea cruises, 1.77 million Americans traveled overseas in 1963. People here were growing more sophisticated about other countries, but it was always nice to come back to a modern American home in the hills (inset photo). The 1963 Cadillac convertible was a great car to catch a ride back home in.

***Advances in Botanical Research** was a brand new journal than began publication in 1963. Among discoveries made that year was the fact that warming the leaves of plants, rather than their roots, promoted faster growth. This nature lover drove a 1963 Cadillac Sedan de Ville to relax in a botanical garden.*

Spending on 1963 advertising and promotions hit a record $12,900,000,000. This ad offered a 1963 Cadillac Sedan de Ville to the winner of DX gasoline's "Parade of Prizes" contest. Even East Germany got into contests, with a factory there offering a Trabant for the best productivity promoting idea.

General Motors was the biggest single advertising buyer. The automaker spent $160 million on advertisements and promotions. This 1963 Cadillac Eldorado is being presented to the winners of a "Buy at Home" contest. At least we assume the winner is pictured, though no one in the photograph looks very happy.

Checker may have based this ad on "Mr. Ed," a hit television show you could watch on a 1963 Philco Cool Chassis TV (inset). The conservative, but roomy Checker did have boxy styling, like the Studebaker Larks that Ed's owner, "Wilburrr" drove. "The Beverly Hillbillies" was the year's top-rated television show.

The world fish catch hit a new high of 46.4 million metric tons. Peru was on top with 6.9 million metric tons and the United States was fifth. These figures did not include very many giant Marlins. As you can see, the 1963 Chevy II Nova 400 station wagon was roomy enough to handle this fisherman's "catch of the day."

About 740,316 people lived in San Francisco in 1963. Some of them saw Herman Prey and Elizabeth Schwarzkopf star in the first production of Strauss' "Capriccio" by the San Francisco Opera. The 1963 Chevrolet Impala convertible was described as the "smoothest way to top off a tour of San Francisco."

The U-2 spy plane that fell in Russia was essentially a powered glider. Gliders hit 70 years-old in 1963. Pioneers Otto Lilenthal, Octave Chanute and Percy Pilcher flew them as early as 1893. Glide ratios indicate the number of units flown before dropping one unit. The 1963 Impala Sport Coupe could glide over a road.

The Disneyland monorail of 1959 sparked the interest of mass transportation planners in the 1960s. A "saddle bag" monorail was built at the Seattle World's Fair and, in 1963, a monorail was erected, in Tokyo, Japan, for the upcoming 1964 Olympics. The 1963 Corvette's new look made it as modern as a monorail.

A distinctive, one-year-only "split window" design was a hit on the 1963 Corvette Sting Ray coupe. A 1960s billboard (inset) promoted Standard Oil Company's Crown Extra gasoline. With a 375 horsepower, optional L-84 engine, the new Sting Ray made "more power to you" more than just a sales slogan.

These skindivers got to the beach in a 1963 Corvair Monza convertible. Diving underwater with scuba equipment, or in a submarine, was dangerous. America discovered this on April 10, 1963, when the United States atomic submarine Thresher and all 129 men aboard were lost on an Atlantic deep water test dive.

With expanded use of undersea cables and communications satellites, direct-distance telephone dialing to any point in the world was predicted in 1963. All of the technological changes kept telephone workers busy. These linemen had one of Chevrolet Truck Division's 1963 "New Reliables" to get to their remote job site.

The luxurious 1963 Chrysler New Yorker four-door hardtop reminds us that the New York Hilton opened that year. The $100 million complex on the Avenue of the Americas was a 46-story building with the city's largest convention facilities.

The 1963 Chrysler 300 Sport Series convertible was a great car to take to Watkins Glen, New York to see English driving ace Graham Hill capture the checkered flag in the United States Gran Prix sports car race.

An economical 1963 Chrysler Newport sedan was great for a family trip to the country. In April 1963, America's farm population was 13.4 million or about 7.1 percent of total population. The number was down 2.3 million from 1960.

Luxury and high-style were things that Chrysler hoped buyers would associate with its upscale New Yorker of 1963. Naturally, a model posing with the car reflected the latest in fashion, including a shift dress, a coat with fur on the inside only, shoes with broader, lower heels and a long, smoothly combed hairdo.

In 1963, Chrysler promoted its luxurious Imperial to specific high-income buyers, such as doctors, lawyers and corporate directors. The latter group deserved a reward for pumping the annual Gross National Product to $588.7 billion, which equated to growth of four percent, even allowing for inflation.

More people got married in 1963, than ever before. The marriage rate that year was 8.7 per 1,000 population. The country had 56 million households and 74 percent were headed by a married man. This 1963 Dodge Polara Sport Coupe was appropriately decorated for this handsome bride and groom's wedding.

After the couple above settled down, they were likely to purchase many of the appliances seen here, for their new home. In 1963, 20 percent of the nation's electric utility companies signed up for the "Gold Medallion" all-electric homes program, which prompted underground residential distribution of electricity.

Compacts, like this 1963 Dodge Dart, grew smaller, but America's buying power went up. Wages increased at over twice the rate of the cost of living. Also, people were only saving about six percent of income, versus a seven percent overall average since 1946. It was hard squeezing more stuff into smaller cars.

Automobiles accounted for 755 billion of the 841 billion passenger miles that Americans traveled in 1963. Here's our Dodge Dart again. As you can see, everything did fit inside, including mom, dad and the boys. With four passengers (the dog doesn't count), it gets four passenger miles for each mile that it goes.

Do you recognize our newly weds from the previous page. This is how they looked, a few years and three kids later. It appears that they took pretty good care of the car and didn't have to use the 50,000-mile warranty too much. However, someone should tell them that a kid's shoes can scratch a hood!

Restaurants benefited from the healthy 1963 economy. This couple visited their favorite eatery in style. Restaurant owners reported that business went up six percent, from 1962. This 1963 Ford Galaxie convertible looks good enough to whet any Ford lover's appetite.

It was easy for kids to get excited about outer space, in 1963, with all that was going on in the United States Space Program. On May15, the Mercury capsule Faith 7, carrying Major Gordon Cooper Jr., was launched from Cape Canaveral, Florida. A young spaceman knows what Galaxy he's in ... the 1963 Ford Galaxie!

Monte Carlo, a French protectorate with a population of 25,000 hosted many visitors in 1963. Earnings from the casinos there stayed high, although gambling revenues saw a decline. One group of visitors brought a 1963 Ford Falcon Sprint hardtop to enter in the famed Monte Carlo Road Rally.

Conservation was a primary concern of zoo keepers in 1963. A Wild Animal Propagation Trust was set up. The Bronx Zoo put 100 acres aside as a Wildlife Survival Center. The parrot-like birds perched on this car may have wound up in that center, but they didn't allow "thunder birds," like the 1963 Sports Roadster.

Engineering News-Record's Construction Cost Index said construction costs stood at 912.14 on September 12, 1963 (based on 1913 as 100 percent). They were 3.7 percent over 1962. One way to keep costs down was a Ford pickup. A cost-effective appliance for any new home was a Culligan water softener (inset).

Home furnishing sales for 1963 were the best in four years, with furniture and home furnishings retailers reporting gains of five percent over 1962. Contributing to the increase was the purchase of new floor coverings. The Ford Econoline van's "knee-high" flat floor made it a great carpet and linoleum delivery truck.

In the ABC federal aid program, more than $1.6 million worth of improvements were done on 17,803 miles of primary and secondary roads and streets during 1963. Of this total, $856,000 came from federal aid funds. Cruising down this smoothly-paved city street is a 1963 International Travelall.

On July 22, 1963, Eugene P. Foley succeeded John E. Horne as administrator of the Small Business Association. The SBA helped small firms, like this laundry service, buy IH Metro delivery vans.

In 1963, magazine advertising revenues rose five percent. Advertising revenues for radio, business publications and outdoor media, as a group, jumped by a smaller three percent. This billboard art shows the "world's most complete line" of trucks, available from International Harvester Corporation.

First class mail went up a penny an ounce (five-cents for letters and four-cents for postcards) on January 7, 1963. Air delivery was three- and two-cents more, respectively. On July 1, Postmaster General John A. Gronouski introduced a new Zip Code system. This carrier had a new right-hand-drive Jeep to use.

According to the United States Department of Agriculture, there were 3.58 million farms in operation here in 1963. The agency's proposal for wheat marketing quotas was defeated by a vote of farmers in May 1963. A stake truck that many farmers did "vote" for was the go-anywhere Jeep FC-170 model.

United States production of flat glass came to nearly $350 million in 1963. Automotive manufacturers were one of the glass industry's biggest markets. The office building behind this1963 Lincoln Continental four-door hardtop also makes extensive use of flat glass in its "open space" architectural design.

In March 1963, heavy rains brought floods to the Ohio River and its tributaries. Rains also ended a long drought in the Gulf Sates, causing flash floods in Georgia. Heavy rains also caused flooding in Washington D.C. and Buffalo in August. The 1963 Lincoln-Continental used galvanized steel for better weather-proofing.

The Apollo Space Program progressed, more or less, on schedule. Its goals included earth-orbital and circumlunar flights and landing a man on the moon. A successful flight of a full-size Apollo command module took place in November. This couple and their shaggy dog are moon-gazing in a 1963 Mercury Comet.

"Ladies love us," read a Standard Oil Company billboard (inset). It recalls the days when you did not have to ask gas station attendants for a key to the restroom. This little lady is checking out a 1963 Mercury Monterey sedan with "Breezeway" ventilation.

Sheraton Hotels opened what was probably the world's most expensive hotel, in Venezuela, in 1963. It cost $30 to $45 million to build. This couple is visiting a fancy hotel in a 1963 Oldsmobile Ninety-Eight. The man may have brought along his Remington Lektronic II (inset), then, the "world's only" cordless electric shaver.

This couple might be heading towards their yacht in their 1963 Oldsmobile Dynamic 88 four-door hard-top. In sailboat racing that year, the yacht Doubloon won the 184-mile Miami to Nassau contest and also took the 40-mile St. Pete to Fort Lauderdale race in Florida.

In 1963, women at the beach often wore visored caps or straw hats. Muumuus, shifts or long T-shirts (called "T-shifts) were also popular beachwear fashions. They were often worn over two-piece bathing suits. America's lowest-priced convertible, the $2,340 Plymouth Valiant, left buyers plenty to spend on clothes.

The Chesapeake Bridge Tunnel was nearing completion in 1963 and, during November, two people walked its entire length. A new $30 million Callahan tunnel into Boston Harbor was being worked on, too. It was targeted for completion in 1966. Cruising through this tunnel is a 1963 Plymouth Sport Fury hardtop.

United States rubber consumption was up to a record 1.75 million long tons in 1963. That was 20,000 tons over the record. No wonder .... both the Harley "Wide Glide" motorcycle (left) and the "Wide-Track" Pontiac Tempest (right) had heftier tires. Of the total output, 45 percent of the rubber being made was synthetic.

The Great Lakes Fishery Commission reported that lake trout from that area were repopulating quickly, after nearly being wiped out by sea lamprey attacks. Perhaps that was good news for this hungry pair pulling up to a seafood restaurant in a 1963 Pontiac Catalina convertible.

In 1963, Jack Nicklaus won $50,000 in the World Series of Golf for the second year in a row. He also took the Masters Tournament, shooting a 286 for the contest. These golfers owned a Pontiac Catalina Safari station wagon. Do you think they drank 7-Up (inset) to help keep them "on the ball?"

This 1963 Pontiac Bonneville Sport Coupe owner is checking a sightseeing guidebook for things to do, while on a "south of the border" vacation. During that year, some 848,000 Americans traveled to Mexico, 631,000 visited the West Indies and Central America and 97,000 went to South America.

These churchgoers went to their house of worship in a 1963 Studebaker Lark. In religious news, a new Roman Catholic pope, Paul VI was elected, after John XXIII died on June 3, 1963. Two Americans, Mother Seton and ex-Philadelphia Bishop John Newmann, were also beatified by the Catholic Church.

According to one reliable source, there was a "startling increase" in air freight in 1963. In fact, total domestic air cargo volume was up 10.3 percent from 1962. A cargo airplane was used to deliver this early Studebaker Avanti coupe to a "long lead" press preview to drum up publicity for the new, fiberglass-bodied car.

1964

A year of little focus, 1964 saw "personality changes" throughout the world. Lyndon Baines Johnson (LBJ) and Hubert Humphrey were elected in America. Khrushchev was disposed in Russia. India's prime minister Nehru died. In Britain, Harold Wilson became prime minister. Elizabeth Taylor married Richard Burton, Jimmy Hoffa went to prison and Malcolm X formed the Black Nationalist party. In February, the *Beatles* made their first visit to America.

Thoughts, philosophies and actions changed, too. The United States Surgeon General blamed lung cancer on cigarette smoking. The CIA discovered "bugs" in the United States embassy in Moscow. China announced it had an A-bomb. Riots and revolts erupted in the Panama Canal Zone, Brazil and Bolivia. Then, North Vietnam attacked American vessels in the Gulf of Tonkin, setting off the biggest powder keg of the decade.

January's big news story was Russia's downing of an United States jet over East Germany. In February, Americans were riding high after the Ranger-6 spacecraft hit the moon and LBJ signed a tax-cut bill. In March, another American jet was down over East Germany. In April, the Worlds Fair opened in New York and General Douglas MacArthur died in Washington, D.C. May brought the sinking of a United States escort carrier, the Card, in Saigon Harbor. In June, the Federal Bureau of Investigation began looking into the murders of three civil rights workers in Mississippi and the Senate passed the civil rights bill.

In July, LBJ signed the Civil Rights Act of 1964, race riots broke out in Rochester, New York and Ranger-7 snapped 4,000 close-up photos of the moon. On August 4, LBJ ordered reprisals against North Vietnam and, three days later, he got a Congressional resolution okaying "any necessary action" there. On September 18, American ships made another engagement in the Gulf of Tonkin and war seemed a certainty. On the 27th, the Warren Commission's report was made public. Reverend Martin Luthur King, Jr. won the Noble Peace Prize in October, the same month China detonated an atomic blast. In November, LBJ took a landslide victory in the United States Presidential Election. In December, a week of flooding in five states left 48 dead and 17,000 homeless. It was not a Merry Christmas in 1964!

On a lighter note, see-through clothing, topless dresses and in-flight movies were new. In the fall, a Saturn I rocket blasted off to start the race-to-the-moon. John, Paul, George and Ringo ... the *Beatles* ... released their innovative, low-budget, black-and-white film, "A Hard Day's Night."

Some of the year's other films included "From Russia With Love," "Dr. Strangelove," "Fail Safe" and "Goldfinger." Small-screen hits included "Peyton Place," "Gilligan's Island," "The Munsters" and "Gomer Pyle."

"Chim Chim Cher-ee" (from the film "Mary Poppins"), "Dang Me," "Leader of the Pack," "We'll Walk in the Sunshine" and "If I Were a Rich Man" were among 1964 hit records. Five other big hits ... "And I Love Her," "Can't Buy Me Love," "Love Me Do," "I Wanna Hold Your Hand" and "A Hard Day's Night" came from the *Beatles*. Stage productions ranged from "Fiddler on the Roof" to "Hello Dolly." In books, the subject matter was just as wide-ranging, running the gamut from sex (in *Candy*) to super-spies (like James Bond in *You Only Live Twice*). In all, 28,451 books were published, an all-time record high.

A number of significant people met their maker in 1964, including actors Alan Ladd, Peter Lorre and Harpo Marx. It was a bad year for singers and songwriters, including Eddie Cantor ("Making Whoopie"), Cole Porter ("Just One of Those Things") and Sam Stept ("Don't Sit Under the Apple Tree"). Ian Fleming, of 007 spy-book fame, was another 1964 statistic. Medal of Honor winner Sergeant Alvin York and Anthony de Francisci, the sculptor who created the "ruptured duck" discharge emblem for World War II vets, were casualties, too. Canada lost Armand Bombardier, inventor of the modern snowmobile. Among deaths in the car world were those of stock car racer Glenn "Fireball" Roberts, on July 2 in Charlotte, North Carolina (after being severely burned in an earlier accident) and Henri Pignozzi, the founder of Simca, who expired on November 18 in Paris, France.

Rambler Classic 770 Cross Country Station

California surfers had it rough in 1964. A tidal wave, caused by an Alaskan earthquake, hit the Crescent City coastal region in March. In December, the "Golden State" was plagued by floods. On rare sunny days, these surfers got to the beach in their 1964 Rambler Classic 770 Cross Country station wagon.

Country and Western music was in. Loretta Lynn got a lifetime record contract in 1962. Merle Haggard's "Sing Me a Sad Song," and "All My Friends are Going to be Strangers" topped the 1963 charts. These musical 1964 Rambler American 440 convertible fans could probably go for a sip of Dr. Pepper (inset).

Hurricane Dora dumped heavy rains from southeast Alabama and Florida to southeast Virginia in September 1964. A Bulova "Warrior" portable radio (inset) could help these 1964 Buick LeSabre convertible owners find shelter from the storm. America's 250,000 amateur radio buffs sent out storm warnings, too.

A mounted policeman warns two Buick Electra 225 owners that a walk in the park could be dangerous. Over 2.6 million serious crimes occurred in America in 1964. The crime rate was 14 serious offenses per 1,000 inhabitants, up three percent. It had grown five times faster than the population rate since 1958.

What surfers wore to the beach in 1964 was collared polo shirts, straight leg pants, denim work shirts, battle jackets, big vinyl ponchos and parkas with an "army surplus" look. What some lucky surfers drove was a 1964 Buick Wildcat convertible with bucket seats and a 401 cubic inch 325 horsepower V-8.

The 1964 Riviera looked like a big Buick on a diet. It combined the marque's traditional feeling of luxury with a trim new appearance. This Riviera owner could maintain her own trim appearance by drinking the Coca-Cola Company's new "single calorie" soda (inset). Called Tab, it had one calories in every six ounces.

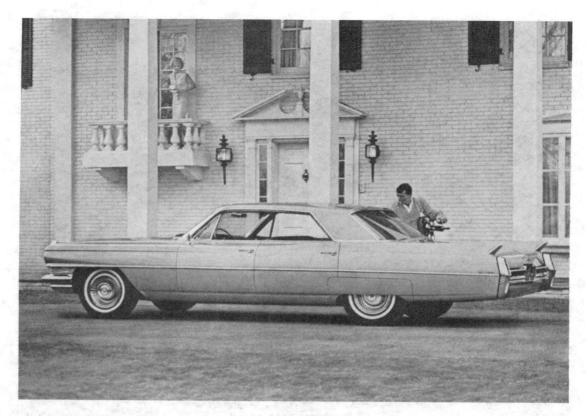

Golfers Jack Nicklaus and Arnold Palmer could both afford a big house and a fancy new Cadillac four-door hardtop in 1964. Nicklaus' combined winnings of $113,286 were $81 higher than Palmer's. It was the first time in history that two golfers had official tournament earnings above $100,000.

Hydroplanes made news in 1964. Donald Campbell's "Bluebird" set a World Speed Record, for water, of 283.60 miles per hour at Lake Dumbleyung, Australia on December 31. An American hydroplane, built by Henry Lauterbach, highlighted this 1964 Cadillac de Ville convertible publicity photo.

In 1964, total personal income of all Americans rose by $28,000,000,000 to $502,000,000,000. However, median personal incomes were up a modest five percent to $6,600. Most folks did not have a door man, a mansion, a sunken living room (inset) or a 1964 Cadillac Fleetwood Brougham four-door hardtop.

New York, New York was a wonderful town. A great car to visit it in was the 1964 Cadillac Coupe de Ville. The city's population stood at 7,781,984 people. On November 21, the world's largest suspension span, the Verrazano-Narrows Bridge, opened between the boroughs of Brooklyn and Staten Island.

A 1964 Chevrolet Corvair Monza in downtown Pittsburgh, Pennsylvania. Real wire wheels were optional, but this car has wire wheel hubcaps. About 604,332 people resided in Pittsburgh in 1964. State Governor William W. Scranton made an unsuccessful bid for the Republican presidential nomination that year.

This 1964 Corvair Monza Spyder ad reminds us that the 17.6-mile Chesapeake Bay Tunnel-Bridge opened in April 1964, after three-and-one-half years. By the way, if the driver squeezes too hard to the left, he may need an "ouchless" Curad plastic bandage (inset), with new Telfa pad, to fix his boo-boo!

*Barry Goldwater's 1964 photo book, **The Face of Arizona**, cost over half as much as a Chevy II Nova sedan. A fund-raising item, the 18 x 14-inch volume had impressive portraits of Indians and landscapes from the Southwest. It cost $1,500. For home photos, Kodak's Instamatic camera (inset) was lots cheaper.*

The 1964 Nova station wagon was a great car to own if you made a household move. Plenty of folks did. Many moved from rural areas to cities. America's farm population was around 7.1 percent of total population, compared to 8.7 percent in 1960. There was 2.3 million less farmers in 1964 than three years earlier.

A 1964 Chevelle Malibu Sport Coupe cruises by a new building. With the strong economy, construction was moving along at a brisk pace. According to one source, the value of new buildings erected in America totaled $65,625,000. Sixty-nine percent were private and 31 percent were in the public sector.

Nationwide receipts for highway work in the United States, by all units of government, reached $13.5 billion during 1964. Of that, about $6.3 billion was spent on new highway construction. The owners of this Malibu hardtop seem quite content to travel California's old Coast Highway to just get away from it all.

In 1964 tennis matches, the United States women's team won at Wimbleton, defeating the British women for the Wightman Cup. However, Australia's Roy Emerson dominated men's tennis there, and in Davis Cup competition. These tennis buffs were fans of the 1964 Chevrolet Impala Sport Sedan.

Like other sports, rock climbing changed in the 1960s. It also started to grow internationally popular. Instead of using steel pistons, which permanently damaged rocks, climbers switched to the use of aluminum chocks. Another internationally popular pastime in 1964 was driving a Corvette Sting Ray coupe.

American retailers did a record $260,000,000,000 in sales during 1964. Two of their big concerns were trading stamps and the leasing of merchandise or service departments. Retailers who were also concerned about product delivery liked the 1964 Chevy-Van's 40 square-feet of flat floor, behind the driver.

With passage of the Wilderness Bill in 1964, the wilderness system gained statutory protection of federal law. Eleven billion board-feet of timber, valued at $151 million, was harvested from National Forests that fiscal year. These 1964 Chevrolet trucks were well-suited to both light- and heavy-duty work in the forest.

For suburbanites, sweaters were fashionable in 1964. They came plain or striped in smooth, ribbed, ruffled, sieve-like or piped styles. While, not a fashion rage, seat belts became standard equipment in the front seat of 1964 cars, like this Imperial convertible. New from Borg-Warner (inset) was the Roll-A-Belt reel.

Herbert Clark Hoover, 31st United States President, died October 20, 1964 at 90-years-old. In law enforcement, another Hoover, J. Edgar, marked his 40th year as FBI head. While not a national figure, Lt. Milton Jenks, of the Michigan State Police Motor Carrier Division, was known to car buffs for his 1964 Chrysler 300 police car. He's now retired in Florida.

The total number of housing starts in 1964 was 1,584,900. That was down 3.4 percent from 1963. Seventy-one percent of the new homes were in metropolitan areas. This new home had a new 1964 Chrysler Sport Coupe parked outside and an old 1924 Chrysler in the garage. Antique car collecting was growing.

At the ninth Winter Olympics, January 29 to February 9 at Innsbruck, Austria, William (Billy) Kidd of Stowe, Vermont and Jim Heuga of Tahoe City, California finished second and third in skiing. It was the first time the United States won any men's skiing medals. Another champ was the 1964 Chrysler Sport Coupe.

INTRODUCING THE DEPENDABLES FOR '64

We didn't invent the compact . . .

we just enlarged upon it!

The original idea about compact automobiles has little similarity to the 1964 Dodge Dart idea.

Now don't get us wrong. Dart certainly is a compact. It parks almost anywhere. It steers quickly, handles lightly. It's about as easy on gas as you hope to get. But from there on out the old idea and the new part company . . . Because the 1964 Dart is a compact in the large economy size!

Dart looks bigger. It sits bigger. It's powered bigger. And at the rear—where luggage belongs—is a vacation-size trunk that's larger than many standard-size cars.

When you add it all up, here's a lot of car going for you. A lot of room and comfort. A lot of durability and service-saving features. A lot of good looks that take you out of the compact class without taking you away from a compact price. '64 Dodge Dart! America's new family-size favorite!

Table-top auto racing was America's big craze in 1964. It began in California, but "Pit Stop" and "Race-A-Rama" signs were appearing in hobby shops coast-to-coast. As you can see, other small cars, like the 1950 Kidillac pedal car, were also enjoyed. Dodge's Dart convertible (bottom) was another popular small-car.

The big fashion news of 1964 was introduction of the topless swim suit and creation of the discotheque dress. Most women, like those in this 1964 Dodge convertible, preferred easy-fitting strapless swimsuits or modified bikinis with boyish little shorts. Shift dresses (inset) were often worn over bathing suits.

Hurricane Cleo hit Florida August 27, 1964 causing heavy rains over a wide area. Cities, like Jacksonville, were declared federal disaster areas by President Lyndon Johnson. Dodge's 1964 styling was far from disastrous. These ladies liked it as much as they liked shopping in the rain (or any weather).

There were 2,367,325 fires in the United States in 1964. Structures were involved in 912,600, which resulted in losses totaling $1,361,500,000. The cost of fires was $1,652,700,000, down 7.3 percent, but over $1.5 billion for the fifth straight year. A hot car was the 1964 Ford Galaxie 500/XL two-door hardtop.

The 1964 Ford Country Squire was advertised as "built to support any population explosion" and "looking young all over." The average size of American households was 3.33 persons, while families averaged 3.71 persons. Half of the population was under 28.3 years old, versus 29.5 years old in 1960.

Tri-level railcars hauling small autos, like 1964 Mustangs, held up to 15 cars. Railroads now hauled 30 percent of the new cars built, versus 10 percent in 1959 and car production was up. This business grew 500 percent in five years. One eastern road had 725 rack cars and made $7.5 million carting 1964 autos.

Benjamin Britten's Symphony For Cello and Orchestra was first performed at the 1964 Aldenburgh Summer Festival. This cellist seems to be interested in performance, too, since he drives a 1964 Thunderbird. Do you suppose that he kept his white convertible tuned-up? Only 9,198 of these cars were built.

In March 1964, there were 56 million American households and 74 percent of them (41.3 million) were headed by a married man whose wife lived with him. In this case, the head of the household got the job of carrying his sleepy-eyed daughter from their 1964 Falcon Squire into the family homestead.

During 1964, America's National Parks played host to about 100 million people. Part of the spectacular Canyonlands of southeast Utah was established by Congress as Canyonlands National Park. A 1964 Fairlane Custom Ranch Wagon carried these campers. Wonder if they were wearing their Keds (inset)?

Home construction was going upwards in 1964. So was the popularity of the Ford F-100 Custom Cab 1/2-ton pickup truck. Independent engineers ran five 1963 Ford trucks 100,000 miles each at the cost of 3.2 cents per mile for gas, oil, tires, preventive maintenance repair.

With a booming 1964 economy, many new home appliances were being retailed. The Ford Econoline Van made a good delivery vehicle. Its low, flat floor required only a 22-inch lift to slide a load on or off.

About 9,336 small airplanes worth $198,500,000 were delivered to private or corporate buyers. This was an all-time record. These 1964 Lincoln-Continental owners could film their friend's solo flight and play it back on a "Private Eye" projector (insert). Keystone Camera's table-top viewer looked like a television.

Art exhibits in Philadelphia (Clifford Still), New York (Jackson Pollock) and Paris (Jean Fautier), made news in the 1964 art world. Jasper Johns' work got a retrospective in New York. This budding young artist is hoping to sell one of his canvases to the driver of a 1964 Lincoln Continental four-door hardtop.

The elegant appearance of the 1964 Mercury Park Lane with "Breezeway" design fits right in with this modern opera house. For 1964, the Metropolitan Opera put on a lavish production of Gian-Carlo Menotti's "The Last Savage" and the New York City Opera premiered Lee Hoiby's "Natalia Petrovna."

At Daytona Beach, Florida, a team of specially-equipped 1964 Mercury Comets ran, around the clock, for 100,000 miles, averaging 105 miles per hour. Later, one of the cars, adjusted for highway use, began a Victory Tour of America. It's shown near a bridge which is not Verrazano-Narrows Bridge, which opened in 1964.

The powerful, 1964 Oldsmobile F-85 Cutlass Sport Coupe was a popular car in the wide open spaces Texas. On September 18, 1964, James Frank Dobie died in Austin. He was an internationally-known folk-lore story-teller and scholar on the Lone Star State. His works included "Tales of Old Time Texas."

The 1964 Olds F-85 wagon had room to carry Peter Kirby, Doug Anakin, Victor and John Emery and their sled. They were members of Canada's gold-medal-winning bobsled team at the Winter Olympics in Innsbruck. A British bobsledder died when his one-man sled crashed. Inset shows a 1964 snow tire.

The only way a real photo could be shot from this vantage point, is from the deck of the Staten Island Ferry, which doesn't have trees! The image of a family going to the New York World's Fair (inset shows the fair's Unisphere) in a 1964 Oldsmobile Vista Cruiser has been superimposed on a photo of Manhattan.

The 1964 Oldsmobile Jetstar 88 Sport Coupe had a top speed of around 120 miles per hour. That's about how fast a skydiver drops from 15,000 to 2,000 feet, before opening his parachute. Higher jumps and lower openings are possible, but not recommended. Skydiving was still considered a rare hobby in 1964.

158

NBC's top television news team got such high ratings for its 1964 Republican convention coverage, that CBS made a staff shake-up, replacing Walter Cronkite with Robert Trout and Roger Mudd. The Plymouth Valiant was featured in commercials on NBC's Chrysler-sponsored hit "The Huntley-Brinkley Report."

Forty percent of the Interstate Highway system, 16,963 miles, were open to traffic by June 30, 1964. During the fiscal year, 2,025 miles of roadway reached full federal standards. Of the $2,400,000,000 spent, $2,100,000,000 was federal government money. Hitting the highway is a 1964 Plymouth Fury station wagon.

Race car driver A.J. Foyt took the Indianapolis 500-mile race, on his way to his fourth United States Auto Club (USAC) championship. A 1964 Plymouth Sport Fury convertible served as official pace car for a race at the "Milwaukee Mile." It was supplied courtesy of North Avenue Plymouth.

Looking a bit like actor Paul Newman in the movie "Hud," a blue-jeaned cowboy struts, with his saddle, towards a 1964-1/2 Plymouth Barracuda. Newman got a 1964 best actor nomination for the 1963 film. Co-stars Patricia Neal and Melvin Douglas won best actress and best supporting actor awards.

As boating enthusiasts, these 1964 Pontiac Catalina convertible lovers probably kept track of the America's Cup action. The United States defender Constellation took four straight races from the British challenger Sovereign in a best of seven contest. It won by comfortable 3/4-mile to two-mile margins.

The 1964 Pontiac LeMans held lots of groceries. America's largest supermarket chain, A & P, saw a big drop in profits. It hiked prices to pay for trading stamp promotions and lost business to competing grocers. How about two pounds of bacon for 89-cents or ground beef for 35-cents per pound!

Pontiac's 1964 Grand Prix fits in at the Winter Olympics in Austria. During the event, three United States athletes got arrested for "stealing" a car they'd borrowed. For resisting arrest, they spent two nights in jail. Two got suspended sentences. New in 1964 was the Polaroid Color Pack camera (inset).

Pictured outside a travel bureau is the 1964 Pontiac Bonneville Sport Coupe. Note the New York World's Fair poster in the window. Paid attendance at the fair for the 1964 season was 27,148,280. Executives predicted that 37.5 million people would visit the extravaganza in 1965, its second and final year.

It's somewhat fitting that Studebaker selected a family of collies to appear in an ad with its 1964 Daytona convertible. Collie may be derived from colley dog, a breed used to herd now-extinct Scottish colley sheep. Studebaker was on the verge of becoming extinct in the middle 1960s and would last just a few years.

One of the leading industrial designers of the 1960s was Brook Stevens, of Mequon, Wisconsin. He styled the 1964 Studebaker Daytona Wagonaire station wagon (left). It had a steel sliding roof that made it easier to carry appliances like a General Electric Mobile Maid dishwasher (right) home from the store.

1965

The "Mod" look, "Op" art and the "Great Society" made 1965 seem a year of labels and buzz words, but bombs buzzing over North Vietnam shrieked the harsh realities of war. United States troop-strength in Southeast Asia grew from 2,500 advisers towards 250,000 fighting men and more Americans died, during one week, than in all of 1964. Men walked in space and scientists saw the first close-up pictures of Mars. A flight around the world passed over both the North and South Poles. Also making news were a ruling requiring health warnings on packages of cigarettes, the enactment of Medicare and the overturning of a Connecticut law banning birth control. In the Northeast, the lights went out one November night. In the South, Martin Luther King's struggle for civil rights continued. The appointment of a black to the United States cabinet contrasted with the outbreak of rioting in Los Angeles, California's Watts section.

January, brought the death of Sir Winston Churchill and poet T.S. Eliot, along with a military coup in South Vietnam. In February, American planes made the first bombing raids into North Vietnam and assassins cut down Malcolm X in New York. March brought the 1965 Freedom March in Selma, Alabama. In April, United States Marines were dispatched to the Dominican Republic when a civil war broke out. The Soviets landed a spacecraft on the moon on May 12. June sent Air Force Major E.H. White on a 20-minute "walk."

In July, United Nations representative Adlai Stevenson passed away. President Lyndon B. Johnson signed the Voting Rights Act of 1965 and a law banning the burning of draft cards. Missionary Dr. Albert Schweitzer, winner of 1952's Nobel Peace Prize, died. A massive power failure, in the Northeastern United States and Canada, "blacked out" the region. On November 27, a peace march brought 25,000 people to Washington, D.C. In December, two American spacecraft rendezvoused in space.

Many famous people met their fate in 1965. Former President Herbert Hoover, Egypt's King Farouk, supreme court justice Felix Frankfurter, financier Bernard Baruch, animal trainer Clyde Beatty, cosmetic company owner Helena Rubenstein and broadcaster Edward R. Murrow were among them. Hollywood lost William Bendix, Constance Bennett, Percy Kilbride, Stan Laurel, Zachary Scott, silent film vamp Mae Murry, Linda Darnell and Clara Bow, plus producer David Selznik. Singers Nat King Cole and Judy Holiday departed, along with "payola" deejay Alan Freed and band leader Spike Jones. Baseball lost Pepper Martin Curly Lambeau, founder of the National Football League, was another of the year's vital statistics.

Among deaths noted in the world of cars was that of Lord William Rootes, who produced the Hillman, Sunbeam and Humber. He passed away on December 12. Stock car racer Billy Wade expired January 5, at Daytona Beach, Florida. Father Devine, the black preacher who founded the Peace Mission Cult and purchased one of the last Duesenbergs, passed away on September 10.

Songs of the year included "It's Not Unusual," "I Got You Babe," "You've Lost That Lovin' Feelin'" and "Mrs. Brown You've Got A Lovely Daughter." Television brought out "The FBI" and "The Dean Martin Show." At the movies, people saw "What's New Pussycat?" "The Agony and the Ecstasy" and "The Yellow Rolls-Royce." The stage came alive with "The Roar of the Greasepaint - the Smell of the Crowd," "The Odd Couple" and "On a Clear Day You Can See Forever." Best-selling books included *The Source*, *Unsafe at Any Speed*, *The Kandy-Kolored Tangerine-Flake Streamline Baby* and *Manchild in the Promised Land*.

All in all, 1965 seemed like a year in which the world needed someone to come to its aid. This was reflected in songs such as "Help Me, Rhonda," the Beatles' song and movie "Help!" Unfortunately, like Don Quixote in the 1965 play "Man of La Mancha" the helpers ... the positive forces in our society ... were busy chasing windmills.

164

Our guess is that they photographed this 1965 Rambler American 440-H hardtop near Point Besie Light, located on the southern end of Manitou Passage. This was to become the last manned light station on the east shore of Lake Michigan. The lighthouse would not be automated until 1983.

The United States government tried to discourage overseas travel in 1965. However, by year's end, travel to Europe rose 14 percent. These travelers got to the dock in a 1965 Rambler American hardtop. Hopefully, the husband packed his Remington Lektronic II cordless shaver (inset) for the trip.

Marlin

There was a drought in New England and the Middle Atlantic states, in 1965. We recall New York City restrictions on swimming and watering lawns. Owners of cars, like this 1965 AMC Marlin, were asked to wash them less. Another suggestion, to shower every other day, helped sales of Avon products (inset).

This AMC advertisement compared hot weather with the 1965 Rambler Classic's hot engine options. During late October, 1965, a record heat wave brought Los Angeles residents temperatures of 90-degrees or better for 10 straight days. This created the worst smog seen there since 1955.

Rather wild fur coats with a youthful, but amusing look were fashionable in 1965. One fashion reviewer described them as being "made from the fur of tame little animals." This up-to-date coat looks like it is *right* in style. So was the owner's 1965 Buick Riviera coupe.

Wouldn't you really rather have a Buick?

The "1965 face" was sculptured with contouring make-up that emphasized bone structure. Also nicely *sculptured* were the feature lines of the 1965 Buick Skylark Grand Sport two-door hardtop. The model's *high-fashion* hairdo looks very much like a popular style by Alexandre, a coiffeur who was in demand.

The Academy of Sciences was Chicago's earliest scientific institution. A new National Arts and Humanities Bill, signed September 19, 1965, gave museums recognition as participants in the nation's arts and humanities movement. Also gaining recognition, by their distinct styling, were 1962-1964 Cadillacs.

In 1965, Congress passed a law requiring cigarettes sold after January 1, 1966 to have a "health hazard" warning. Many American men began smoking pipes. This pipe-smoking 1965 Cadillac Coupe de Ville owner watched the six-year-old, number one hit, show "Bonanza" on his RCA color television (inset).

The 1965 Chevy II Nova Super Sport Coupe was a great little car to bring a new baby home in. During 1965, live births dropped under four million for the first time in 12 years. About 3,767,000 occurred. The birth rate of 19.4 per 1,000 citizens was down from 21.2 in 1964.

Paul Bunyon would be wowed by the 11.24 billion board feet of lumber, worth $161 million, cut from national forests in 1965. That was some 25 percent of all American lumber. A proud father and son pose with a 1965 Chevy II wagon. Junior's trimmed mustache (inset) was likely a beard by the end of the 1960s.

In 1965, geologists discovered fossils two billion years old in the rocks of the Gunflint Foundation, on the North shore of Lake Superior. The owners of the 1965 Malibu Sports Coupe visited a rock formation, too, but only to relax, cool off and have some fun.

Rain, rain go away. In the summer of 1965, heavy rains fell in the Southeast and other areas. In Denver, precipitation caused $100 million in flood damages. Sometimes, an umbrella did little good, as this 1965 Malibu Sport Coupe driver discovered. She needs a General Electric clothes dryer (inset) for just $99.95.

General Motors said the 1965 Corvair Monza Sport Sedan's styling had "international flair." On the international scene, Italy's Felice Gimondi won the Tour de France bicycle race on July 14. Bicycles were starting to get popular here, as were small motorcycles, like the $225 Harley M-50 (inset).

A 1965 Corvair Monza convertible was set in an Irish sheep pasture to highlight Chevrolet's "international" ad theme. Actually, the leading wool producers were Australia (1.694 billion pounds); the Soviet Union (727 million pounds) and New Zealand (650 million pounds). There were about 986.3 million sheep worldwide.

In 1965, the removal of excise tax on items like furs, luggage, jewelry, handbags and toilet preparations stimulated their purchase and apparel sales climbed three percent, too. It looks like this 1965 Chevrolet Impala Sport Sedan owner took advantage of the lower prices and got a smooch as his reward.

The telephone poles behind this 1965 Corvette Sting Ray coupe bring to mind that America had 88 million phones in use that year. In fact, in 1965, the United States had an average of one million people talking to each other on their telephones every hour of every day of the year.

The personal, per capita, pretax income of farmers (from farm sources) rose sharply in 1965, reaching nearly 30 percent above the 1964 level. That meant many farmers had money to invest in equipment like a 1965 Chevrolet Fleetside pickup truck. Overall, farm production expenses rose significantly, too.

In 1965, skilled construction workers, such as bricklayers, carpenters and iron workers, averaged $4.96 per hour in wages, a 4.5 percent increase, while common labor wages dropped six percent to $3.41. Using economical Chevrolet trucks at a job site was a way to keep building costs low.

Newport 4-Door Hardtop

Fourth of July fireworks highlighted an "explosion" of interest in the popular-priced 1965 Chrysler New-port four-door hardtop. Just in time for the holiday, Title VII of the Civil Rights Act of 1964 went into effect July 2, 1965. It was the first national law prohibiting discrimination against minorities in employment.

The number of children under 14 years old jumped 5.6 percent in 1965. These kids probably watched baseball games (inset), on television, with mom and dad. Commercials on sports programs brought American broadcasters about $140 million. A sporty 1965 car was the Chrysler New Yorker two-door hardtop.

Neil Simon's "The Odd Couple" was a Broadway hit of 1965. There's nothing odd about this couple's taste in automobiles. The 1965 Dodge Polara two-door hardtop was a good-looking, reliable vehicle. With its low price tag, there was probably enough money left to visit the theater box office and get tickets.

The 1965 Dodge Custom 880 Station Wagon was a handy model for dog lovers who took their pets with them. There was room in the back for two large dogs, plus durable vinyl upholstery. A Scottish terrier named Champion Carmichael's Fanfare took top honors at the Westminster Kennel Club's dog show in 1965.

Dodge promised buyers "lots new" in its hot 1965 Dart GT two-door hardtop. This car may have been at a state fair or a bigger one. Two-year attendance at the New York World's Fair was announced as 51,607,037 people, topping the previous high of 44,932,978 for the 1939-1940 New York World's Fair.

Steeplechase racing turned 100 years old in 1965. It had been introduced into the United States, from Canada, in 1865. The first steeplechase race in this country was held in Paterson, New Jersey. This rider seems to be interested in another "thoroughbred" ... the 1965 Dodge Monaco two-door hardtop.

Home building volume continued above the 1.5 million level in 1965. Total non-farm housing starts in the fiscal year were 1,531,000, a six percent decline from 1964. A hard-working truck for home builders was the 1965 Dodge D100 Sweptline pickup.

Many of the record 110 million people visiting National Parks and Monuments during 1965 were youths involved in scouting. This group of Boy Scouts arrived at their remote campsite in a 1965 Dodge A100 van.

The trucking industry grossed $10,000,000,000 in revenues during 1965. Volume was up, but profits fell, due to higher costs. Dodge sold this NL-1000 Tilt-Cab diesel for over-the-road hauling. Its short cab permitted longer trailers.

177

The United States' female population increased 8.1 percent between July 1, 1960 and July 1, 1965. These young ladies were part of the increase and also helped explain the growth of station wagon sales. The 1965 Ford Falcon Squire was one of the fanciest small station wagons on the market.

Hughes Aircraft Corporation won a government contract to built the United States Army 714 Light Observation Helicopters at $19,860 each, excluding cost of the engines. Civilian helicopters were more expensive. Those who couldn't afford a "whirlybird," could buy a 1965 Thunderbird. It was only $4,394.

Since 1960, there had been only a six percent gain in the number of American families consisting of related persons living together. However, the number of families with a head of household living alone or living with non-related people jumped 21 percent. This family got around in a 1965 Ford Fairlane wagon.

In June 1965, the 20th anniversary meeting of the United Nations was held in San Francisco to commemorate the signing of the UN Charter there. The city was also featured in an ad for the 1965 Mustang convertible. It joked of the owner getting lucky after buying the car, saying he won the city in a faro game.

In 1936, England's Duke of Windsor gave up his throne to marry an American divorcee. On March 15, 1965, Queen Elizabeth II met the Duchess of Windsor for the first time since 1936. A 1965 Ford LTD also faced up to a blue-blooded Briton, proving to be quieter than a Rolls-Royce at 60 miles per hour.

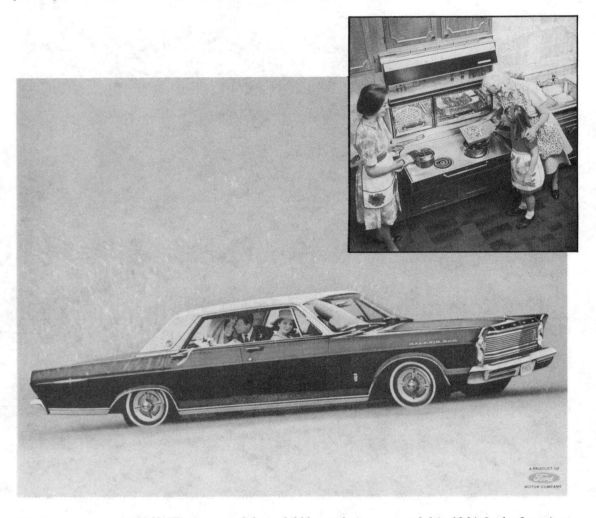

Marriages went up in 1965. The rate was 9.3 per 1,000 population, versus 9.1 in 1964. In the first nine months, that meant an increase of 42,000 nuptials. These newlyweds sped away from the church in a Galaxie 500/LTD four-door hardtop. They wanted to rush home and try their new electric range (inset).

Railroads earned $10,900,000,000 hauling freight in 1965. This represented a five percent increase over 1964 and a record high in peacetime. They handled about 43 percent of all types of shipments in America. This 1965 Ford F-150 Custom Cab pickup just finished fetching a load of cartons from a freight train.

"Bonanza," NBC's six-year-old Western, continued as America's number one television show in 1965. A new series called "Wild, Wild West" was about secret agents operating in the Old West. Tending to its own rodeo and cowboy chores is a 1965 Ford F-100 Styleside pickup featuring Twin-I-Beam suspension.

211 cu. ft. load space. Up to one ton payload. Only 168" long. Specify a 4 cyl. 90 h.p. engine or a 6 cyl. 140 h.p. engine. Turns inside a 38-ft. circle. It also turns heads.

This 1965 GMC Handi-Van looks like it was hijacked and robbed of its cargo. The crime rate was up five percent in 1965. Burglaries and larcenies involving over $50 went up six percent, while the auto theft rate climbed four percent. One positive change was in captures of FBI fugitives. They went up by 681 to 13,491.

How to get to a fish dinner

The Bureau of Sport Fisheries and Wildlife was trying to save the Apache trout from extinction in 1965. The primary threat to this beautiful, bright gold and olive-green fish wasn't sportsmen, like these 1965 International Scout owners. The Apache trout were being wiped out by indiscriminate use of pesticides.

During February 1965, most of the country (except the West and Florida) was gripped by extreme cold. Blizzards paralyzed the Great Lakes region, blocking roads and causing schools and businesses to shut their doors. The owner of this 1965 International 4 x 4 pickup truck kept busy keeping driveways plowed.

In 1965, the Coast Guard Auxiliary was active in 826 flotillas nationwide. Its 23,000 volunteers checked 183,000 boats. They instructed 138,000 boaters on the proper and safe way to operate their craft. The four-wheel-drive 1965 Jeep Wagoneer, with optional "Vigilante" V-8, was a great tow vehicle.

*It took substantial resources to start up a children's theater or drive a Lincoln Continental. The darker car is a 1965 sedan and the lighter car is a 1967 sedan. In 1965, the **Village Voice** presented a special citation to an acting troupe called The Paper Bag Players for raising the level of children's theater.*

These United States Marines were lucky to draw honor guard duty for the VIP owner of this 1965 Lincoln Continental. Many of their comrades were heading to South Vietnam, where American armed forces grew from 23,500 advisers, in January, to nearly 200,000 combat-ready troops, by year's end.

Olympic medalist Bill Kidd, of Colorado University, dominated the North American Ski Championships in 1965. He helped Colorado's team become National Collegiate Athletic Association champs. This 1965 Mercury was the courtesy car for special guests at Squaw Valley Lodge in Tahoe City, California.

Growing interest in antique cars was reflected by two of 1965's top movies. "The Great Race" was a parody of the first around-the-world auto race and "The Yellow Rolls-Royce" was a romantic drama. This 1965 Mercury Comet Caliente two-door hardtop dropped in at a Concours d' Elegance.

Trading volume on the New York Stock Exchange set a record of 1,558,266,262 shares. The Dow -Jones Index of stock prices went from 874.13 in January to 969.26 on December 31. That meant that it was a good year for sales of more expensive cars, like this Oldsmobile Starfire two-door hardtop.

Jets were in the news in 1965. Grumman Aircraft Engineering Corporation announced plans to produce a new $2.1 million business jet called the Gulfstream II in 1967. Oldsmobile continued a long-time tradition of using aviation names for its high-performance products. Here's the 1965 Jetstar 88 convertible.

Some songs these "minstrels" might be playing, include the 1965 hits, "Hang-On Sloopy." "Help Me, Rhonda," "Stop! In the Name of Love," and "Wooly, Bully." Their beach party transportation was a 1965 Plymouth Sport Fury convertible.

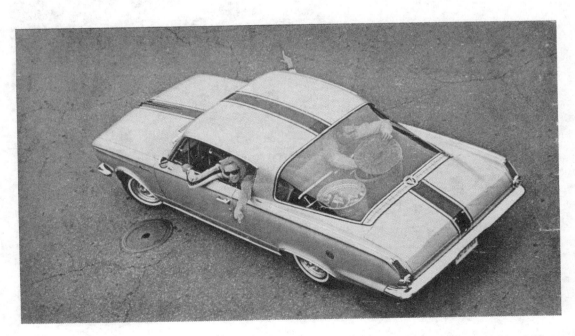

In 1965, the average American family spent about 18.5 percent of its take-home income for food. That compared to 21.6 percent in 1955. This gang has the storage area behind the folding rear seat of their 1965 Plymouth Barracuda fastback loaded with good things to eat and drink at a family picnic.

Le Corbusier (Charles Edouard Jeanneret-Gris), the pioneering Frenchman who championed the use of curved and irregular shapes in modern architecture, passed away on August 27, 1965 at age 77. The 1965 Plymouth Valiant two-door hardtop sported a modern design and the best price of any compact car.

Jean Claude Killy, the French downhill skier, won his first combined World Championship Skiing title in 1965. It was a prelude of what was to come for the then 22-year-old athlete. Plymouth advertised the Fury Sport Coupe as the car to take, when busting out of town, for the ski slopes, on Friday afternoon.

America's top-ranked tennis star, in 1965, was National Clay Courts title winner Dennis Ralston. Nancy Richey, the nation's leading female player, took the Women's National Clay Courts title. A leader in the automobile world was the 1965 Pontiac Grand Prix Sports Coupe.

A tiger was probably safer away from zoos in 1965. The Cheyenne Mountain Zoo, in Colorado Springs, and the Crandon Park Zoo, in Key Biscayne, were damaged by a flood and Hurricane Betsy. Over 252 animals died in the Florida zoo. The Pontiac GTO "Tiger" (on right) was based on the Tempest LeMans (on left).

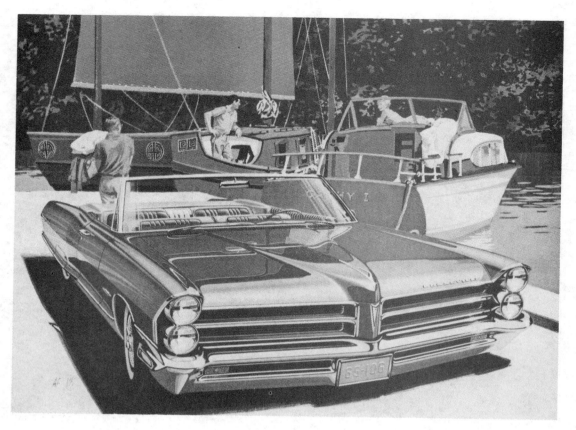

A modern power boat is moored next to a Chinese junk. Also "moored" nearby is a Pontiac Bonneville convertible. In 1965, Red China set off its second atomic explosion. Friction between Red China and the Soviet Union continued, while China's "brotherly" unity with North Vietnam was internationally played up.

Assateague Island National Seashore, the largest undeveloped seashore between Cape Cod and Cape Hatteras, was authorized for the National Park System in 1965. It was in Maryland and Virginia, far from the heavily-developed seashore that this 1965 Pontiac Catalina convertible is parked near.

Focusing on safe driving, several new traffic laws were passed in 1965. One North Carolina measure out-lawed embraces behind the wheel. A new Florida law made it illegal for monkeys to drive! Did the man in this 1965 Studebaker Lark Daytona hardtop yield before entering the highway?

A 1964 Studebaker Lark Daytona convertible served as pace car for a 1965 stock car race at the Milwau-kee State Fairgrounds. It was supplied by Crazy Jim's Motors at 906 South 16th Street. Freddie Lorenzen was the winner of the Daytona 500 that year. Scotland's Jimmy Clark took the Indy 500.

1966

Mass murders in America. Bombs in Vietnam. Floods in Florence (Italy). Cultural revolution in China. Army coups in Argentina. Guerrilla warfare in the Middle East. Upheaval in Africa. The Monkees on television. Violence, terror, turmoil and tragedy were part of 1966. Mini-skirts were in, along with "granny" glasses. Some ladies preferred pant suits, others see-through dresses. Undressed-on-top waitresses served food in some restaurants. Others still refused to serve customers of all races. America put spacecraft on the moon and Venus, but kept Ralph Ginsberg's *Eros* out of book stores. In politics, Senator Everett Dirkson broke his leg and Senator Edward Brooke, of Massachusetts, broke the color barrier. The strongest auto safety legislation cleared Congress.

Crime ran rampant in America. Illinois Senator Charles Percy lost his daughter to a killer. Black freedom marcher James Meredith was gunned down in Mississippi. Drifter Richard E. Speck murdered eight student nurses in Chicago and sniper Charles J. Whitman shot 15 people at Texas State University. Meanwhile, the supreme court's Miranda decision "handcuffed" police.

January started with a crippling New York transit strike and ended with renewed bombing of North Vietnam. February's big story was a military coup in Ghana. In March, another riot broke out in Los Angeles. An American H-bomb lost off the coast of Spain during 1965 was recovered in April 1966. That was the good news. Then, in May came reports that Buddhist students had burned a United States cultural center in South Vietnam. On June 28, Argentina's president Arturo Illia was overthrown.

Racial violence rocked Chicago in July. In August, Aleksei Kosygin was re-elected Soviet Premier. An election was held in South Vietnam in September. In October, 12 firemen died in New York City. November brought the worst floods that Italy had seen in centuries. In December, Red China set off its fifth nuclear device. The United States and Russia signed a treaty barring nuclear weapons in outer space.

Who died in 1966? The nation mourned Walt Disney. The art world lost sculptors Jean Arp and Alberto Giacometti. Several important World War II military leaders died, including Admiral Nimitz and United States Army Generals Joseph W. Stillwell and Richard K. Sutherland. Retailing lost Sebastian Kresge, of five-and-dime store fame, and Bernard and Fredric Gimbel. "Ike's" secretary of state, Christian Herter, was another statistic, as were gossip columnist Hedda Hopper, comedian Ed Wynn and golfer Tony Lema, who crashed in a plane. While some may win and some may lose, baseball's "Sad" Sam Jones had held records for both, with 228 big league victories and 218 defeats. He passed away July 6. Singers Helen Kane (the "boop-boop-a-doop" girl of the flapper era) and Sophie Tucker died, as did actors Gertrude Berg and Montgomery Clift and silent film stars Francis X. Bushman and "Buster" Keaton.

Two significant automakers perished. Jean-Pierre Peugeot was grandson of the French firm's founder and its savior after World War II. He became director of Peugeot in 1922 and died October 18, in Paris. In America, we lost Alfred P. Sloane, Jr., the legendary General Motors master planner who served as president of the company from 1923 to 1937 and chairman of the board from 1937 to 1956.

New to television were "Mission: Impossible" and "Family Affair." Running down some top 1966 movies, we have "Dr. Zhivago," "The Russians Are Coming," "Blow Up" and "Who's Afraid of Virginia Woolf?" Top songs were "Born Free," "Eleanor Rigby," "California Dreamin'" and "A Groovy Kind of Love." "Batman," "Mission Impossible" and "Family Affair" bowed on television. On the stage, "A Lion in Winter" was playing and "Cabaret" was packing them in. Books of the best-seller list ranged from *Valley of the Dolls* to *In Cold Blood*.

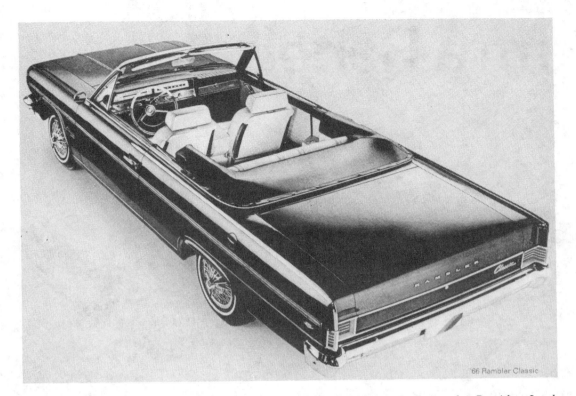

Convertibles, like this 1966 Rambler Classic, seemed to be an endangered species after President Lyndon B. Johnson signed the National Traffic and Motor Safety Act and Highway Safety Act on September 9, 1966. Over 50,000 people died on the highways that year.

New York City started 1966 with a Transit Workers strike that affected some six million commuters. Mayor John Lindsay didn't get a settlement until January 13. The 1966 Rambler Classic 770 Cross Country three-seat wagon would have been a great car for New York commuters during the strike.

I'm a Rebel!

"He's a Rebel!" was a popular hit song of the 1960s and American Motor's used the headline "I'm a Rebel!" to sell the 1966 Rambler Classic Rebel two-door hardtop. It was available with a zoomy 327-cubic-inch V-8 and a roomy bucket seat interior.

for a party of six!

In 1966, over half the people in the country were under 25-years-old. They liked cars with sporty, air-craft-inspired designs like AMC's Marlin fastback. Even younger Americans were tuned in to the new trend. Mattel's streamlined X-15 tricycle (inset) was promoted as "a jet on wheels."

Only 30 percent of Americans, including these 1966 Buick Electra 225 owners, lived in rural homes. More people lived in cities. Chicago's Marina City (inset) was designed, by Bertrand Goldberg Associates, as circular apartment towers with shops, restaurants, a skating rink and a swimming pool.

In 1966, University of Arizona researchers studied tree rings from 1860 to 1962 in an attempt to reliably date trees by the number of rings in their trunks and better understand forest ecology. This Buick Special coupe may hit that tree, if the driver doesn't slide behind the steering wheel.

Devastating Italian floods caused $2,500,000,000 in damages on November 4-5, 1966. Some $15 million in artworks were flooded. Jackie Kennedy was chairman of the U.S. Committee to Rescue Italian Art. This 1966 Cadillac Fleetwood sedan might well have been seen at a charity fund-raiser.

*A charming old railroad station belies the fact that commuter lines tested high-speed trains in 1966. The Long Island Railroad had its Turboliner. The New York Central's jet-car, with twin gas turbine engines, went 183.85 miles per hour. A 1966 Cadillac Convertible de ville was **not** quite that fast!*

It was the year of the dress in women's fashions. Dress styles included "Skimps," "Puptents" and "small-dresses." Large, bold geometric patterns, including polka dots, were in. A dressy-looking car with squared-off, geometric styling was the 1966 Chevy II Nova Super Sport.

On June 1, 1966, the population of Canada stood at 19,919,000. Many Canadians drove Acadian automobiles, which were Chevy II clones. Lester B. Pearson was Canada's Prime Minister and George P. Vanier was governor-general. There was a Canadian national rail strike on August 26.

The sport of hot rodding entered a boom period in the mid-1960s. It had started in the early postwar years, when prewar cars were modified for racing on California dry lakes. The introduction of muscle cars, like this 1966 Chevelle SS-396 Sport Coupe, widened the spectrum of interest.

*The National Park Service marked its 50th year with release of an anniversary postage stamp, at Yellowstone Park, August 25, 1966. Interest in camping inspired the new magazine **Outdoors Calling**. A 1966 Chevrolet wagon was handy for camping. So was Chiffon's "soft tub" margarine.*

Housing starts were down 19 percent from 1965, as record "high" mortgage rates (up to seven percent in some places) made getting money difficult. It was much easier to get a 1966 Chevrolet Caprice station wagon, since car prices went up only 7/10 of a percent.

Spy shows were hot. Chevrolet pictured a spy (inset) with its fastback Sport Coupe. Noel Harrison starred in a new spoof called "The Girl From U.N.C.L.E." and "Secret Agent" was a hit for Patrick McGoohan. "I Spy" won Bill Cosby an Emmy. Are the Chevrolet Impala wagon owners spies, too?

An old English sheep dog named Champion Fezziwig Raggedy Andy was international best of show winner in 1966. Champion Zeley Moore Maida Magic, a wire fox terrier, won the Westminster Kennel Club's top honor. These dog lovers found their 1966 Corvair to be a perfect "Collie car.".

*The 1966 Corvette Sting Ray coupe was a car for winners. Frank Robinson, 31-year-old Baltimore Orioles outfielder, won the Corvette that **Sport** magazine presented, annually, to the World Series hero. The "Birds" took the series, from the Los Angeles Dodgers, in four straight games.*

The 1966 Chrysler Newport Sport Coupe was a favorite with book worms. Over $2,500,000,000 in book sales was rung up in 1966. Best sellers were Harold Robbin's **The Adventurers**, *James Michener's* **The Source**, *Bel Kaufman's* **Up the Down Staircase** *and Jacqueline Susann's* **Valley of the Dolls**.

The 1966 Newport Sport Coupe was also a "hot ticket" with firefighters. According to the National Fire Protection Association, an average of 1,569 homes were damaged or destroyed by fires daily, in 1966. The blazes caused $1,016,400 in damages and claimed 18 lives per day.

A cool soft serve and a dip in the ocean went great with a 1966 Chrysler Newport convertible on a hot day. Ice cream got more expensive, along with other dairy products, when milk prices took an 11 percent leap in the summer. More cattle were being slaughtered for meat, which limited dairy production.

Even the school dunce could tell the 1966 Newport was just a few dollars a month costlier than most small cars similarly equipped. Enrollment in United States schools totaled 56 million in 1966, a 2.6 percent gain. This included some six million in college, 13 million in high school and 37 million in grade school.

During 1966, the top fencing team in the National Collegiate Athletic Association was one from New York University. Like the 1966 Dodge Coronet 500 hardtop, they looked "sharp" and "foiled" all of their competition to get to the "point" of the matter.

While considered a compact car, the 1966 Dodge Dart GT convertible had plenty of leg-stretching room. Another spacey machine of the same year was Frigidare's Gemini 19 refrigerator-freezer (inset). It featured a power capsule billed as a "space age successor to the old-fashioned compressor."

The 1966 Dodge Coronet 500 convertible was a great car to own during the summer of 1966. There were heat waves everywhere. Washington D.C. had 63 straight days above 90 degrees in July and August. Fresno, California experienced 19 consecutive days above 100 degrees in late August!

An aircraft-inspired look characterized the first 1966 Dodge Charger. This fastback coupe kept "flying," even after five major airlines went on strike July 8, 1966. The walkout of machinists at Eastern, National, Northwest, TWA and United, lasted 43 days.

Under the Water Quality Act of 1965, the government and American Public Works Association contracted to create a blueprint for action against emptying waste into streams and lakes. The 1966 Ford Galaxie 500XL looked great in this rural setting. So, would a MerCruiser powered speedboat (inset).

A Ford Galaxie 500XL may not have been such an unusual sight in Switzerland in 1966. The country's 5,900,000 citizens were enjoying full employment and foreigners, including Americans, were needed to fill jobs there. They made up one-third of the work force. Swiss women got the right to vote in 1966.

Stowe, Vermont hosted the United States Ski Championships, March 18-20, 1966. The French won six titles. Guy Perillat and Jean-Claude Killy were the top male skiers, while Marielle Goitschel and 16-year-old Florence Steuer were female stars. A ski rack was optional on the 1966 Fairlane GTA hardtop.

In college football, a 1966 rivalry pitted Notre Dame against Michigan State. Their final regular season game drew the largest television audience for college games up to that time. Some 33 million viewers watched them battle to a 10-10 tie. The 1966 Ford Country Squire wagon (left), offered football players' parents enough room to bring their family to the East Lansing, Michigan stadium. Those who didn't come, could watch on a Zenith, black-and-white, 21-inch compact portable television (right).

Four weather satellites were launched by the United States in 1966: the ESSAs 1, 2 and 3 and the Nimbus 2. The latter could snap 3,000 photos a day, to spot lightning and other dangerous atmospheric conditions. As flashy as an electrical storm was the 1966 Thunderbird Town Landau.

The "youth market" got attention in 1966. Kids 18-years-old and under spent an average of $11.50 per week. They bought toys, entertainment, hobby supplies and sports equipment. A motorized Mustang GT toy was available for $4.95 from Ford dealers. The Show 'N' Tell phono-viewer (inset) was also popular.

Ford aimed ads for the 1966 Mustang Sport Coupe at middle aged men. One such person who was in the public eye was Dr. Timothy Leary. In 1966, after the hallucigen drug LSD was outlawed, Leary founded the League of Spiritual Discovery. He described it as "an unorthodox psychedelic religion."

Ford said that a 1966 Mustang would make this young shopper "the sweetheart of the Supermarket Set." Supermarket prices climbed four to five percent. Hamburger was up 7.2 percent , bread went up nine percent and milk rose 11 percent. Some women set up picket lines to protest high prices.

Average weekly earnings of workers in the construction trades climbed from $143.34 in 1965 to $149 in 1966. Their average work week, in August, was 36.9 hours, versus 37.3 hours for the same month in 1965. This carpenter brought along a helper to "drive" his 1966 Ford "Twin-I-Beam" pickup.

The United States Travel Service promoted tourism to America. Director John W. Black used the theme "Festival USA '66" to highlight local events nationwide. Some 1.2 billion foreign visitors were expected to spend an average of $395 each here. These tourists saw the USA in a 1966 Ford Bronco.

Many historic treasures were saved in 1966. President Johnson made 14 areas eligible for landmark status, including the Monhegan Islands off Maine, the Great Swamp in Morris County, New Jersey and Cape Lookout National Seashore in North Carolina. An historic car is the 1966 Lincoln Continental.

Despite anxieties over rising interest rates (5.5 percent) and other factors, the banking industry prospered in 1966. Profits rose slightly and interest in bank credit cards began. The government also liberalized merger regulations. A "banker's car" was the stately 1966 Lincoln Continental limousine.

A 1966 Mercury Colony Park wagon is seen at Palm Springs, California's Racquet Club. Tennis teacher Joe Subek, of Greenwich, Connecticut, is unofficially recognized as racquetball's inventor in 1950. Full rules weren't codified until 1968. Thomas Pugh, of England, took the 1966 U.S. Open racquets title.

The links at Pebble Beach, California, along with Saint Andrews in Scotland and Augusta National, in Georgia (site of the annual Masters tournament), are considered the most famous and difficult of golf courses. This 1966 Mercury hardtop served as a courtesy car for the elegant Del Monte Lodge at Pebble Beach.

France's Marielle Goitschel and Austria's Karl Schranz were big skiing champs during the Warner Cup Races, March 24-26, 1966, at Sun Valley, Idaho. This 1966 Mercury was a courtesy car for special guests visiting the Sun Valley Lodge. It featured a 428-cubic-inch V-8 and "Stereo-Sonic" eight-track tape system.

Sport fishing was enjoyed by 28,000,000 Americans. About $7,535,000 was generated, by excise taxes on fishing tackle, to support fish hatcheries. A new magazine called Sport Fishing was launched that year. The big Colony Park and compact Comet Villager were 1966 Mercury wagons that fishermen loved.

Cable cars were San Francisco's most famous form of mass transit in 1966. However, the California toll bridge authority was authorized to issue $47,000,000 in revenue bonds to use in building a rapid transit tube under San Francisco Bay. The 1966 Oldsmobile Jetstar 88 hardtop was perfect for the city's steep hills.

Postmaster Larry O'Brien reported mail volume, for 1966, was up 5.5 percent, to 75.8 billion pieces. This was despite a cost of $1 for long-distance calls to any point in the United States after 8 pm Sundays (inset). Some such calls cost half as much as they did in 1950. This mailer is driving a 1966 Oldsmobile Jetstar 88.

Prices for meals at restaurants rose an average of five percent during 1966. However, we can't specifically document that this applied to lobster dinners at the Fisherman's Grotto, in San Francisco. The car is the same 1966 Oldsmobile Jetstar 88 Sport Coupe that seemed to get around, all over the town.

Highway construction in America hit a record in 1966. Some 103 million licensed drivers went 900 billion miles on 3.7 million miles of roads. Another 2,174 miles of the Interstate system were opened, bringing the total to 21,570 miles. The 1966 Oldsmobile Toronado hit the road to front-wheel-drive technology.

In both men's and women's fashions, the "military" look, with rows of buttons marching down the front of coats and jackets, was one of many popular styles. The 1966 Plymouth Sport Fury two-door hardtop also had a patriotic look, with its red, white and blue trim bars.

The cost of living in the United States rose 3.7 percent between October 1965 and October 1966. Despite a gradual wage increase, purchasing power dropped one percent. That made it harder for this couple to meet the monthly mortgage on their big house and payments for their Plymouth Fury four-door hardtop.

About 900,000 military personnel and 356,000 civilians worked for the United States Air Force in 1966. The strength of its tactical fighters, reconnaissance aircraft and air-warfare forces reached record levels in the Vietnam war. A fighter appeared in photos with Plymouth's "Hemi Under Glass" Barracuda drag racer.

World consumption of rubber in 1966 was 5,735,000 long-tons, an increase of eight percent. The United States was the biggest customer for both natural and synthetic rubber products. One reason was that the pavement-scorching 1966 Plymouth Satellite "street hemi" was very good at "burning rubber."

Pontiac's 1966 Catalina 2+2 was a fast car. Fast on water was Mira Slovak, 1966 hydroplane champion. In February, Skeeter Johnson went 89.064 miles per hour in his Wa Wa Two. Three hydroplane pilots, Rex Manchester, Don Wilson and Ron Musson died in one regatta. Chuck Thompson was killed in another.

This 1966 Pontiac Grand Prix Sport Coupe appears to be cruising the streets of Florida. The state had a population of 5,941,000. The earliest hurricane seen in 15 years hit Florida in June 1966. Hurricane Alma caused $5 million in damages and five deaths. Later, it brought much-needed rain to the Northeast states.

More Americans were boating than ever before. During 1966, the United States Coast Guard answered 43,466 calls for assistance and saved $3,633,250,900 worth of property and cargo. It rescued 2,629 persons from peril. In peril of losing his heart to a lady convertible owner was a 1966 Pontiac Catalina admirer.

The 1966 Pontiac Bonneville Safari wagon was a rich-looking "beach buggy." Experienced skin divers would have had an easy job becoming Navy "frogmen" that year. The Vietnam war strained the navy's resources, even though its 1966 manpower level of 750,000 was above the 728,000 projected for 1967.

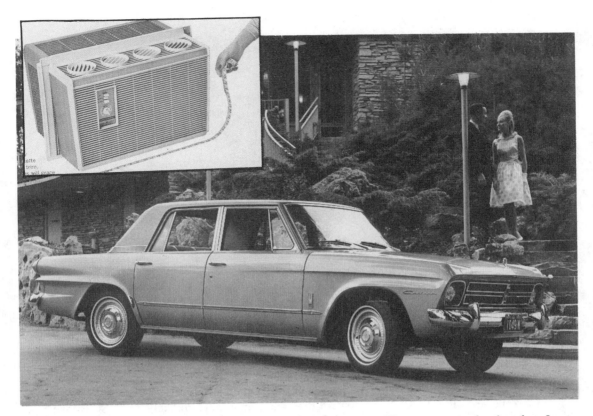

General Electric's Fashionette air conditioner (inset) had a Duramold outer case made of modern Lexan that was beautiful and virtually impervious to weather. Studebaker had failed to keep its products up-to-date, like General Electric. The 1966 Lark Daytona sedan body had elements that dated back to 1953.

After a profitable first half, with a net of $8.3 million, Studebaker declared its first stock dividend since 1954. However, late in 1966, the company's automotive operations "sailed" into history. This move ended 114-years of building transportation vehicles from prairie schooners to 1966 Lark Daytonas.

1967

The "Twiggy look," a heart transplant and the Mariner 5 space craft passing Venus, were some of the exciting changes associated with 1967. The year began with LBJ asking Congress for an income tax surcharge. No wonder it ended with Congress passing an anti-poverty bill!

In 1967, Americans heard "All You Need is Love" and Simon & Garfunkel's "59th St. Bridge Song (Feeling Groovy)." Glenn Campbell's "By the Time I Get to Phoenix" competed with Arlo Guthrie's folk tune "Alice's Restaurant" for record sales. It was a year of contrasts. Movies championed heroes (British spy James Bond in "Casino Royale") and villains ("Bonnie & Clyde"). Glamorized soldiers starred in "The Dirty Dozen." Real-life crime was the focus of Truman Capote's "In Cold Blood." "There's a Girl in My Soup" and the all-black cast version of "Hello Dolly" were Broadway productions, while books read by Americans included *The Arrangement*, *Rosemary's Baby* and *Death of a President*.

It was getting hard to separate good from bad. Russia clashed with Red China, Stalin's daughter defected, an Israeli plane bombed an American ship and anti-war protesters became a majority, as Vietnam's "body count" rose above 100,000 in October.

Every month was news-filled. In January, the United States, Russia and 58 other nations agreed to limit military activity in space. A fire killed three Apollo astronauts at Cape Kennedy. In February, police caught Boston's strangler and Congress approved the 25th amendment. March saw union leader Jimmy Hoffa sent to a "pen" in Pennsylvania. In April, General William Westmoreland predicted victory in Vietnam and boxer Cassius Clay nixed being drafted. A Russian cosmonaut died when his capsule crashed upon re-entry. May saw United States planes dropping the first bombs on downtown Hanoi. In June, Israel won the Six-Day War and Thurgood Marshall became the first Negro on the Supreme Court.

Riots erupted in Newark and Detroit. Michigan governor, ex-American Motors head George Romney, called out the National Guard. Other July news included a deadly fire on the U.S.S. Forrestal in Vietnam and a rail strike ended by LBJ. By August, 45,000 more troops were Vietnam-bound. LBJ upped his tax surcharge. The United States Public Health Service issued a report on the perils of smoking. On Aug. 19, black radical H. Rap Brown was jailed on a gun charge. Six days later, American Nazi leader George Rockwell fell to an assassin. September brought riots in Milwaukee. Nguyen Van Thieu was elected president of Vietnam. In October, United Auto Workers struck Ford and Egypt struck Israel, sinking one of its destroyers. The Mariner 5 space probe passed Venus and the St. Louis Cardinals passed Boston's Red Sox in the World Series. Devaluation of the British Pound, on November 18, shocked the world. In politics, Cleveland's Carl Stokes became the nation's first black mayor. Eugene McCarthy announced his bid for president. In December, the Concorde supersonic jetliner was unveiled.

In 1967, acting lost Nelson Eddy, Bert Lahr, Jayne Mansfield, Claude Rains and Spencer Tracy; the art world lost Edward Hooper, Rene Magritte and Carl Sandburg; politics lost Konrad Adenaur and Clement Attlee; publishing lost Henry Luce; and religion lost Cardinal Francis Joseph Spellman. Other notable deaths included "Monopoly" game inventor Charles B. Darrow; folk singer Woodie Guthrie; and Beatles discover Brian Epstein. Jack Ruby, who shot suspected JFK assassin Lee Harvey Oswald, died in prison and playboy millionaire Tommy Manville departed the world and 11 ex-wives. Automotive personalities meeting their fate included British race driver Donald Campbell (whose hydroplane crashed at 300 miles per hour on January 4); Henry J. Kaiser (who built ships, Hoover Dam and Kaiser cars) on January 27, in Paris, France; and pioneer automaker J. Frank Duryea.

In 1967, there were 97.5 million cars in the United States. Four out of five families had a car in their garage and 14 million of them had more than one. Some even had a couple of Rambler Americans. A Huffy "Rail" bicycle was another item stored in many garages in 1967.

Ringling family control of The Ringling Brothers and Barnum and Bailey Circus ended in 1967, when the show was sold to a group of businessmen. That same year, Gene Plowden wrote the book **Those Amazing Ringlings and Their Circus**. This 1967 Rambler American Rogue hardtop visited the circus.

A 1967 AMC Ambassador climbs a steep hill in San Francisco. Many of the 742,855 residents there watched their city become a focal point of popular music, thanks to groups such as The Jefferson Airplane, The Grateful Dead, Mobey Grape and Big Brother & The Holding Company.

In 1967, the United States Post Office handled 79.1 billion pieces of mail, a 4.7 percent annual increase. A 13 percent hike in international mailing rates, the first since 1961, was put into effect on May 1. It was not related to the use of economical 1967 Ambassadors as mail delivery cars.

Canadian motels enjoyed a boom, as that nation became the top choice of American travelers. A record 12.25 million tourists and 23 million over-and-back visitors came to see the United States Pavilion (inset) and other Expo 67 attractions. These tourists drove a 1967 Buick GS-400 convertible.

Spending on construction rose four percent, to $77 billion, in 1967. Commercial buildings, like the structure behind this 1967 Buick Riviera, consumed $6.825 billion of the total, a one percent decrease. Rising building costs were a big reason the total went up, rather than more activity.

Some politicians "sat on the fence" during a lengthy debate over extending the military draft. The measure finally passed June 20. It added four years, but restricted the president's ability to change the draft system. It was easy to catch another kind of draft in a 1967 Buick Wildcat convertible.

According to the National Highway Safety Bureau, American car makers conducted 91 recalls, to check for and repair mechanical defects, during the 12 months ending September 9, 1967. These campaigns involved 1,800,000 vehicles. Factory servicemen check over a two-year old 1965 Buick Wildcat.

Television Westerns (inset) tried a comeback and failed. NBC's "Virginian" and "High Chaparral" were 14th and 48th, respectively, in Neilsen's ratings. ABC's "Guns of Will Sonnett" was 35th. "Gunsmoke," on CBS, tied for 23rd. This Western theme ad featured Cadillac's 1967 Coupe DeVille and Eldorado.

This 1967 Cadillac convertible might be departing the city behind it for good. With 70 percent of Americans living on one percent of the nation's land, perhaps urban riots were inevitable. In 1967, there were 75 major riots with over 18,000 deaths or injuries. Their cost was estimated at $664.5 million.

Tight money conditions of late 1966, caused banking industry losses in 1967. To get lending money, banks hiked interest rates as high as 5.5 percent. Things improved in late-1967 and the truth-in-lending law was also passed. Truthfully, the 1967 Cadillac Eldorado looks "just right" in front of a bank.

New York City launched crack downs on crime, prostitution and illegal parking. In Manhattan, near the St. Regis Hotel, parking fines doubled and the infamous Tow-Away Program was stepped up. This Coupe DeVille may be bringing art fans to the city's midtown galleries to see an "Op Art" (insert) exhibit.

Early in 1967, the United States reached agreements with Japan and the Soviet Union to extend America's offshore fishing jurisdiction from three to 12 miles. The owners of this 1967 Chevelle Malibu convertible were unlikely to sail out as far as commercial fishermen, in their search for a catch.

The 1967 Chevelle Malibu hardtop was a great car to drive to your favorite surfing spot and an Admiral 13-transistor portable AM/FM radio (inset) was handy for musical entertainment at the beach. In 1967, Australia's Nat Young took the World's Men's Surfing Championship.

Jack Nicklaus took a first, second and third in 1967's four biggest golf tournaments. He missed only on the Masters, which was won by Don January. The top woman golfer was Lou Dill, of Deer Park, Texas. This golfing couple got to the local links in a 1967 Chevy II Nova Super Sport Coupe.

Congress added 22 areas to National Parks in 1967. Hearings were held on establishing wilderness areas in six national parks, three national monuments and a national historic park. These folks are heading into the wilderness with their 1967 Corvair 500 and Anscomatic 126 instant-loading camera (inset).

Bell Telephone created an experimental "lineless" phone. It operated like today's cordless phones, with a range of 100 to 1,500 feet. A 1967 Camaro SS Sport Coupe owner uses a pay phone to order tickets to see Phil Silvers (inset) in the Broadway play "A Funny Thing Happened on the Way to the Forum."

General Motors was the second largest advertiser in the United States in 1967. It spent $208 million, while number one Proctor & Gamble bought $265 million worth of ads. Few ad dollars were used to promote the 1967 Corvette Sting Ray Sport Coupe, which represented the last year of a styling cycle.

The 1967 Caprice Custom Coupe.

The Boeing 737 short range twin jetliner made its maiden voyage in 1967, a year that 130 million airline passengers took to the skies. There were 1,100 jets, 400 turbo props and 500 piston aircraft in service with commercial carriers. A high-flying car of the year was Chevrolet's Caprice Sport Coupe.

Watch Dan Blocker, Michael Landon and Lorne Greene, stars of Chevrolet's "Bonanza," on NBC-TV next Sunday night.

In 1967, television was carried by 766 stations to 70 million Americans in 57 million homes. The top-rated Western was "Bonanza," with Dan Blocker, Michael Landon and Lorne Green. It ranked seventh in the Nielsen ratings. Chevrolet pushed sales of 1967 Impalas and Bel Airs with a "Bonanza Sale."

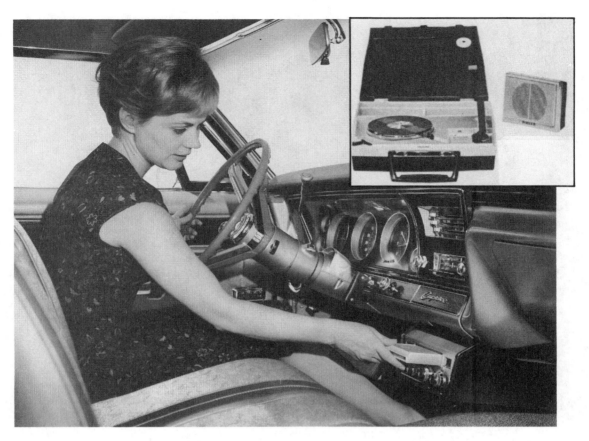

Eight-tracks were optional in 1967 Caprices. This music fan could be playing the Beatles' "Sgt. Pepper's Lonely Hearts Club Band," Bobbie Gentry's country ballard "Ode to Billie Joe," or Janis Ian's protest song "Society's Child." A battery-powered stereo (inset) was another portable music machine.

National Park visits hit a record 133 million in 1967. One way to go was in a 1967 Chevrolet pickup with a Wolverine Camper. A four-year total of federal recreation areas showed that, for the first time in years, more land was set aside for preservation than home developments, shopping centers or highways.

Para-sailing was an exciting new recreational sport that was evolving in 1967. It was depicted in an advertisement for the 1967 Chrysler Newport four-door hardtop. Chrysler sponsored the "Bob Hope and The Chrysler Theatre," in color, on NBC-TV every Wednesday night.

The 1967 Chrysler 300 Sport Coupe was promoted as "a special car for special people." Skydiving was still a fairly "special" hobby that year, although it got some negative national publicity on Aug. 27, when 16 skydivers perished after plunging in to Lake Erie, near Huron, Ohio.

These skin divers emerged from their underwater playground to find a 1967 Chrysler Newport Sport Coupe parked on the beach. Speaking of underwater, on Aug. 3, 1967, it was announced that Commander Scott Carpenter would resign as an astronaut to prepare for 1968's SeaLab III underwater survival project.

The 1967 Imperial Crown convertible was a real "land yacht." A sleek 12 meter yacht designed by Olin Stephens and skippered by Emil (Bus) Mosbacher, Jr. took four straight victories over Australia's "Dame Pattie" to win the America's Cup in September 1967. The New York Yacht Club's Intrepid kept the record of never giving up the cup since 1851.

The mid-1960s was the era of racing and high performance and "Dandy" Dick Landy helped Dodge promote sales of its muscle cars. When he wasn't racing a pair of Coronet R/T hardtops, the drag star conducted special performance clinics at Dodge dealerships throughout the country.

Seven million domestic cars and 700,000 imports sold in America in 1967, a 15 percent drop from 1966. Sales of clothing, like this model's coat, went up seven percent. Food merchants saw a one percent boost in sales. Increased popularity of Swanson frozen dinners (inset) contributed to the rise.

The first major redesign of Ford's Mustang "pony car" came in 1967. Among real "ponies," Damascus, an undersized three-year-old son of Sword Dancer, won a record $817,941 to become the richest race horse. He won the Belmont Stakes, the Preakness and 10 other races, but ran third in the 1967 Kentucky Derby.

On June 10-11, 1967, a Ford Mark IV prototype, with chassis of lightweight, high-strength, honeycomb aluminum, took a runaway victory in the grueling 24 Hours of LeMans. Driven by A.J. Foyt and Dan Gurney, it set a record 135.48 mile per hour pace. Foyt also got $171,237 for winning the Indy 500.

Increased home building pushed home furnishings and appliance sales up over five percent in 1967. A cigar-smoking gent visited the furniture store in a shopping center with his 1967 Ford XL hardtop. A truck that visited shopping centers to promote a new Canada Dry drink was the "Winkmobile" (inset).

Ford's 1967 Galaxie 500 jumped a steeplechase, but 1968 models didn't leap off assembly lines once the United Auto Workers struck Ford September 7, 1967. It closed for 60 days at a cost of 600,000 vehicles. The final settlement, the union said, would give veteran workers $5,000 to $6,000 per year for life.

The "Mod" look was in for 1967, as a fun-with-fashions attitude swept the clothing business. Old uniforms, military capes and other kooky outfits, such as sweaters with racing stripes, were in vogue. Racing stripes were also very fashionable on the 1967 Ford Fairlane "390" GT Sport Coupe.

School enrollments jumped, in 1967, for the 23rd year in a row. There were 37 million elementary school and 13.7 million high school students. Teacher salaries averaged $6,821. A 1967 Falcon took this lad to school, where he saw audio-visual presentations from an Airequipt 400 series projector (inset).

W.W. Butterworth was United States Ambassador to Canada. A. Edgar Ritchies represented Canada here. Both diplomats viewed Expo 67 with interest. The world's fair drew 50.3 million visitors to Canada. Some came in 1967 Falcon Sport Coupes, while others saw Air Canada's catchy ads (inset) and flew.

The first four-door Thunderbird arrived in 1967. Among its standard benefits was a Tilt-Away steering wheel that automatically moved out of the driver's way when he or she entered the car. For a new model, this was a popular body style. It drew 24,967 buyers.

The 1967 Fairlane Ranchero was a "horse of a different color." The sedan-pickup used to be based on the Falcon. Buckpasser, horse of the year in 1966, was syndicated for a record $4.8 million. After the Woodward stakes, he was retired to stud as the third highest money-winner ($1.462 million) in history.

In Canada, a Hydro-Quebec construction program was creating one of the largest dam of its kind. Called "Manic 5," it was to stretch 4,000 feet long, rise 703 feet high and generate 1.3 million kilowatts of energy. Ford's tough 1967 F-series Styleside pickups were well-suited for work on such jobs.

The average production worker in manufacturing earned $116.28 per week, up $2.15 from 1966. People earning $15,000 per year were considered "affluent." Those who enjoyed "The Continental Life" could afford riding lessons for their daughter and a $5,795 Lincoln Continental four-door sedan.

In general aviation, about 13,000 new single and multi-engine airplanes were delivered to private and corporate users in 1967. This was down from the 15,768 sold the previous year. Also down, by over 4,700 units, was the production of Lincoln Continental two-door hardtops.

Despite a mild recession, Americans shopped 'til they dropped in 1967. Consumers put $315 billion in merchant's cash registers, up four or five percent. Stores had a good Christmas season, with total sales of around $5 billion. These holiday shoppers drove a 1967 Comet Caliente four-door sedan.

Surrounding a 1967 Mercury Comet are America's safest young drivers. During the first 10 months of the year, 276,338 Americans took the National Safety Council's defensive driving course. As of November 1, over a half million had done so, but accidents were the leading cause of death of persons one to 37.

Mercury said drivers back from a 600-mile trip in a 1967 Mercury Brougham would feel comfortable. Americans averaged 10,000 miles of driving per year; a cumulative total of 1 trillion miles. Government efforts to encourage American to travel at home prompted 140 million travelers to spend $26 billion here.

*Mercury's entry in the "pony car" market was a "cat car" called the Cougar. It captured **Motor Trend** magazine's "Car of the Year" honors in 1967. Seen here is the XR-7 model, which featured soft glove leather upholstery, an overhead console, full instrumentation and walnut-grained vinyl interior trim panels.*

America had about 2.5 million skiers in 1967. A a ski week package with meals, lodging, lift tickets and lessons was about $80. Ski boots cost $25 and fiberglass skis $100. Most skiers were college grads with $15,000 incomes. No wonder Oldsmobile used skiing as a theme for its 1967 Vista-Cruiser wagon ads.

A new $1.2 million art collection at the Virginia Meadows Museum, on the campus of Southern University, was comprised mainly of works by Goya (1746-1828), a Spanish artist who painted many bullfighting scenes. Since it was nicknamed the "Toro," Oldsmobile used a bullfighter in this 1967 Toronado ad.

The United States Coast Guard didn't have to rescue these 1967 Plymouth Belvedere Sport Coupe owners when their homemade barge sank. However, it did answer 29,832 calls for search and rescue operations in 1967. They involved vessels and cargo with a total value of more than $2.3 billion.

Best of Show in 1967 international dog shows was Champion Salilyn's Aristocrat, an English springer spaniel. In national events, Champion Bardene Bingo, a Scottish Terrier, was the top-ranked dog. Another top-ranked beauty seen at this dog show was the 1967 Plymouth Sport Fury two-door hardtop.

Under a 1967 recommendation by Wyoming and the National Park Service, 2,500 hunters were licensed, by the state, to take part in an elk-reduction program. Grand Teton was the only National Park in which animal control by this method was permitted. These hunters may have been looking for elk or some other species, but they wound up "bagging" a 1967 Plymouth Sport Fury instead.

Plymouth called its full-size Fury suburban a "crew-size" wagon and pictured it with a nine-member rowing team. The 1967 Intercollegiate Rowing Association champs were from Pennsylvania. The Vesper Boat Club, of Philadelphia, was ranked as top United States team. "Check the styling," said Plymouth. "It's a fine car enlarged upon, not a panel truck with windows."

Arnold Palmer was first to pass the all-time $1 million plateau of total money won in golfing, in his 13-year career. However, his 1967 earnings were $182,915, second to the $261,567.66 that Jack Nicklaus won that year. Another big winner with the golf course set was the 1967 Pontiac Catalina Sport Coupe.

At the 1967 Pan-American Games, held in Winnipeg, Canada, a group of teen-age swimmers led by 17-year-olds Mark Spitz and Claudia Kolb won 28 gold medals. A "gold medal winner" with swimming buffs was Pontiac's 1967 Bonneville Sport Coupe. A 400 cubic-inch V-8 engine was standard equipment.

The United Nations General Assembly designated 1967 as "International Tourist Year." Travel to Europe increased about 10 percent from the 1.525 million travelers of 1966. Pontiac's one-year-only 1967 Grand Prix convertible had a European flavor that made it look right at home there.

To the South, Mexico attracted an increased number of American tourists. Over 1.5 million visitors from the United States spent some $545 million there. The Olympics, scheduled for Mexico City in 1968, accounted for part of the increase. These tourists drove down in their 1967 Grand Prix ragtop.

1968

The year 1968 was a busy one. Liberal reforms in Czechoslovakia were crushed by Soviet troops. Constitutional government returned to Greece. Portugal replaced its dictator, Salazar. In France, Charles DeGaulle made concessions to stay in power. In America, LBJ said he didn't want power. England "bit" the economic "bullet," while the crew of the U.S.S. Pueblo faced bullets when North Korea captured them.

In Vietnam, Hanoi launched the Tet Offensive against Saigon, during a "truce." At Khesanh, 5,500 allied troops were besieged by 20,000 North Vietnamese. Israelis and Arabs clashed in the Middle East. In Africa, starvation, caused by civil war with Nigeria, killed thousands in Biafra.

American's watched history unfold on television. Assassins gunned down Martin Luther King, Jr. and Robert F. Kennedy. Race riots lit up many cities. Inflation burned investors. Astronauts orbited the moon. Richard Nixon won in a three-way race for the White House. The 1968 campaign was most remembered for anti-war protests and police brutality at the Democratic National Convention.

Julie Nixon wed David Eisenhower and Lynda Bird Robb gave LBJ his second grandchild. Ice skater Peggy Fleming won at the Winter Olympics at Grenoble, France. At Mexico City's Summer Olympics, American S. John Carlos and Tommie Smith caused a stir with a "black power" salute during the "Star Spangled Banner." Rowan & Martin made the country "Laugh-In," while Tiny Tim tried to bring out smiles, too. In Sylmar, California, construction began on J.J. Nethercutt's San Sylmar museum with a prestigious collection of classic cars.

North Korea's Pueblo piracy and the Tet Offensive headlined January. In February, "Tricky Dick" Nixon announced his candidacy. March saw a Martin Luther King-led labor protest, in Memphis, Tennessee, erupt into violence. King was shot and killed on April 4, after returning there. On May 11, blacks converged on Washington, D.C. to erect a "Resurrection City," as part of the "Poor Peoples' Campaign." Robert F. Kennedy was shot in Los Angeles, on the night of June 5. He died the next day.

In July, Pope Paul VI underlined a position against birth control. Soviet troops invaded Czechoslovakia in August. September brought a crackdown on student demonstrations in Mexico and the downing of the 900th U.S. plane over North Vietnam. In October, LBJ announced a halt in the bombing of Hanoi. Jackie Kennedy married Aristotle Onassis. Nixon was elected in November. In December, three astronauts orbited the moon; the Pueblo crew was released; Arabs attacked an Israeli airliner in Athens, Greece; and Red China set off its fifth nuclear explosion.

Hits heard in 1968 included "Hey, Jude," "Little Green Apples" and "Harper Valley P.T.A." New television shows included "Julia," "Here's Lucy" and "Hawaii Five-O." Big screen hits ranged from "Bullitt" and "2001: A Space Odyssey" to "Rosemary's Baby" and "Planet of the Apes." The Beetles had another hit with "The Yellow Submarine." Stage productions included "Hair" and "Zorba." On bookshelves, titles like *Airport*, *The Electric Kool-Aid Acid Test* and *Myra Breckinridge* were found.

Kennedy and King lead a parade of personalities passing away in 1968. Others included writers Helen Keller, Edna Ferber, Upton Sinclair and John Steinbeck; motion picture stars Tallulah Bankhead and Ramon Novarro; and British film director Anthony Asquith, who did "The Yellow Rolls-Royce." Artist Adolf Dehn, scientist Otto Hahn (who discovered nuclear fission in 1939) and Soviet cosmonaut Yuri Gargarin (in an airplane crash) were other statistics. In the world of auto racing, Scotland's Jim Clark was killed in a crash at Hockenheim, West Germany on April 7. He was the first British driver to capture the checkered flag at the Indianapolis 500-Mile Race.

Race driver Craig Breedlove (right) took one of American Motor's new AMX two-seaters to the Goodyear Tire Company test track in February 1968. He proceeded to establish 106 World Speed Records. Approximately 50 replica "Craig Breedlove" AMXs with red, white and blue paint jobs were then built.

The recreational vehicle industry was hot throughout the 1960s. Travel trailer shipments to dealers went up every year from 1960 (when they were at 40,300) to 1968 (when they hit 153,650). American Motor's 1968 Ambassador station wagon made a great tow vehicle, especially with a 343 cubic-inch V-8.

There was lots of room in the 1968 Rambler 770 wagon, but filling it grew harder. Consumers saw the largest cost of living jump since 1951. The Consumer Price Index went up four percent. Price hikes on items a wagon might carry were 4.5 percent on food, 5.5 percent on furniture and 6 percent on clothing.

*Automotive News, Roominess Index, 1968.

American families this size weren't common in 1968. Population growth was two million per year, compared to three million per year in the early 1960s. The birth rate was down to 17.4 per thousand. Some kids born early in the decade were almost ready for their first Smith-Corona portable typewriter (inset).

In the 1968 Olympics in Mexico City, American equestrian William Steinkraus won a gold medal for equestrian jumping. A fellow equestrian appeared in this advertisement for Buick's mid-size car. With its standard 230-horsepower V-8 engine, the 1968 Skylark Sport Coupe could also "jump" pretty well.

Power Boaters outnumbered sailors eight-to-one, but sailing was getting popular in 1968. Schools run by the Red Cross, U.S. Power Boat Squadrons, yacht clubs and civic groups were turning out thousands of new sailors per year. Mrs. Graham Brown, a sailing enthusiast, had a 1968 Buick Sportwagon. Sailing was highlighted in an ad (inset) for the Maganavox "Aegen Classic" television.

Housing starts in 1968 totaled 1.49 million, a hefty 13 percent increase over 1967. Spending for private residential building was up 19 percent at $28.2 billion. John Magno, a construction engineer from New York, told Americans, "This is my first Buick, but it won't be my last."

The United States continued leading all areas of the free world in automobile registrations for 1968. It had 51 percent of the total with 101,600,000 registered vehicles. Of 60.2 million households, 78 percent owned a car. Among 22.1 million owning multiple cars was this 1968 Buick Riviera owner's family.

Cadillac Motor Division set its fourth consecutive record for sales in 1968 and achieved it despite a 21-day United Auto Workers' walkout at the Fisher Body Fleetwood plant, in Detroit, in November 1967. One reason for growth was a line expanded to 11 models, led off by the Convertible DeVille.

"Predicted log contests" were popular with boaters in 1968. They involved the Skipper predicting how long a 25-mile course would take him to navigate, then trying to match the prediction without using a watch. The Skipper on the left seems very interested in navigating his way to a 1968 Cadillac Sedan DeVille.

In 1968, Zack Willson, Jr. won the All-around Casting Championship for the second consecutive year. This angler seems to be "casting" for opinions about the 1968 Cadillac Coupe DeVille. Most likely, the car owner gave him a glowing report of Cadillac's performance and durability. They were great cars.

The domestic travel industry took its first steps to close the "travel gap," offering foreign tourists an assortment of discounts on air fares, car rentals and hotel rooms. The American Banking Association also canceled a group flight to Europe. This 1968 Eldorado owner is taking off on a business trip.

Op art and pop art were crazes of 1968 and, naturally, wound up as inspirations for ladies' fashion trends. "Mini" hemlines and ankle boots complemented the youthful new look of this shift-dress. The 1969 Chevy II Nova coupe also had a youth-oriented image with a long hood and short rear deck.

The year 1968 brought a major advance in prices for restaurant meals and snacks consumed away from home. Eating sandwiches, fries and malts at a rural country roadside eatery was still quite economical, though. One of the year's top economy V-8s was the 1968 Chevy II Nova coupe with the "307" small-block.

By June 30, 1968, about $4.2 billion worth of work was underway or authorized on federal-aid primary, secondary and urban roads. Funds came from the states and federal government on a 50/50 basis. A 1968 Camaro SS-350 Sport Coupe was perfect for reaching a rustic hillside home (inset) via this winding highway.

About 152.9 million people came to National Parks during 1968. That was a 5.5 percent increase from the previous year. On Oct. 2, the National Park System consisted of 268 areas totaling 28.7 million acres. Chevrolet's mid-size Chevelle station wagon was a top-rated family camping vehicle.

Both clothing and cars evolved into youthful new designs in the '60s. The all-new, 1968 Corvette Sting Ray Coupe was a far cry from the original 1953 model (see our book **The Fabulous '50s***). Men's sportswear had also changed from the 1930s (inset left) to Fortel's "Mr. Leggs" sportswear of 1968 (inset right).*

A 1968 Caprice coupe by the Golden Gate Bridge. Spans nationwide were inspected by the government, in 1968, after a disaster in December 1967. The Silver Bridge, in Point Pleasant, West Virginia, collapsed completely, with no warning, under a load of Christmas traffic. It plunged into the Ohio River.

These 1968 Chevrolet wagons (Caprice Estate, in front, and Chevelle Nomad Custom) could haul a lot of folks to amusement parks, like two new ones in Texas. Houston's "Astroworld," cost $20 million. The second entertainment park was part of "HemisFair '68," an international fair held in San Antonio.

Boating generated retail expenditures of over $3 million yearly. Over eight million boats were owned by Americans. They included five million outboards, 600,000 inboards, 600,000 sailboats and two million rowboats, dinghies, canoes and other craft. A 1968 Chevrolet C10 pickup hauled a rubber raft with ease.

Comedy and football fans saw a lot of Chryslers in 1968, including this sporty 300 convertible. The auto-maker sponsored both "The Bob Hope Show" and American Football League (AFL) games on NBC-TV. In the 1968 Super Bowl, New York's Jets beat the Baltimore Colts 16-7, boosting the AFL stature into the big leagues.

This beauty had a dazzling appearance. The same can be said for the 1968 Chrysler New Yorker two-door hardtop that she's walking away from! Ladies' haircuts and beauty shop services climbed some six percent in price, prompting many women to use Clairol True-to-Light makeup mirrors (inset) at home.

If the home behind the 1968 Dodge Coronet 500 wagon belongs to its owners, they were definitely living above the "poverty level." More and more Americans were. The total number living in poverty had gone from 38.9 million in 1959 to 29.7 million in 1966. Poverty was defined as a family of four or more with income below $3,380.

In team competition at the 1968 Olympics, the Canadian equestrian team took the gold medal. Many spectators photographed the action with a Kodak Polaroid camera (inset), which sold for under $50. Another award winning thoroughbred was the 1968 Dodge Monaco Sport Coupe.

Chrysler Corporation had an excellent year in 1968. Its net rose to $14.9 million, from $6.7 million the previous year. Profit margins soared to four percent, up from 2.2 percent in 1967. One reason for the improvement was the popularity of the company's muscle cars, like the 1968 Dodge Coronet 500.

On April 8, 1968, first lady, Lady Bird Johnson, dedicated the largest National Seashore. The Wild Barrier Islands, along the coast of Texas, were preserved in the Padre Island National Seashore. This 1968 Dodge Charger was pretty wild-looking with a new "Coke Bottle" semi-fastback body.

Many American workers "moved up the ladder" in 1968, as the military draft depleted the size of the available work force. As a result, female workers found new opportunities for higher wages and better jobs. Some invested their salary increases in the "little-bit-fancier" 1968 Ford Falcon Futura sedan.

In May 1968, heavy rains fell in Ohio, causing serious flooding in the southern part of the state. Over 3,000 persons were evacuated from their homes and the region suffered $9 million worth of property damage. The power disc brakes offered on the 1968 Ford Fairlane were of a water-resistant design.

Ford prospered in 1968, following 1967's strike. Earnings rose to $391 million, from $267 million, and the profit margin was up to 5.1 percent. Average monthly payments on cars like the 1968 Country Squire, Country Sedan and Ranch Wagon were slightly above the $91 average for all cars.

This 1968 Ford two-door hardtop could have been photographed in Rome or Greece. The latter country was an archaeological Mecca in 1968. In one dig, researchers uncovered luxurious Roman baths in ancient Corinth. Each room was lined with colored marble and each bath had up to four heated pools.

The 1968 Ford XL was a great road car and this one looks like it's traveling an Arizona highway. On September 23, 1968, the Lord Mayor of London, Sir Gilbert Inglefield, was a visitor to Lake Havasu City, a new community where the London Bridge was being reconstructed as a tourist attraction.

A new distance-measuring device called a laser-geodimeter, was tested in 1968. It measured distance precisely by calculating the time it took for a coherent light beam to travel to and from an object. Lighting up the personal-luxury car market were the 1968 Thunderbird four-door Landau and two-door Landau.

Sidney, a white-shirt-and-tie sort of guy, stopped sea shelling at the seashore after getting his 1968 Mustang Fastback GT. According to an ad, he became a lifeguard and saved three bathing beauties. In Olympic swimming, 16-year-old Debbie Meyer, of California, became the first woman to win Three gold medals.

Offbeat entertainer Tiny Tim (Herbert Khaury) was a long-haired, 40-year-old "flower child" whose falsetto rendition of "Tiptoe Through the Tulips" hit a responsive chord in 1968. The 1968 Mustang convertible parked outside Pedal Pusher Flowers, was "planted" firmly in the sports-compact car marketplace.

A surveyor used his 1968 Ford F-250 Styleside pickup with four-wheel-drive to reach remote sites. The cost of land in the United States was increasing at an average of 15 percent a year in 1968 and represented 22 percent of the cost of homes or apartments. This contributed to the nation's housing shortage.

The number of eight-cylinder trucks built in America crested the one million mark for the first time in 1968. One reason for the popularity of V-8 engines was that more power was required for trucks with camper units. Ford's F-Series pickups came with engines up to 390 cubic inches.

Parked outside a church-like structure is a 1968 Continental Mark III coupe. In May of 1968, the National Federation of Priest's Councils formed in Chicago, Illinois, with Reverend Patrick O'Malley as president. Small churches were able to purchase Hammond Organs, (inset) with prices starting at $595.

Not all tree lovers were happy when the 58,000-acre Redwood National Park was established in 1968. The Sierra Club and other conservationists favored a 90,000-acre site in the same Humboldt/Del Monte County region. The trees behind this 1968 Continental Mark III are much smaller than giant redwoods.

A federal travel tax on European trips was pushed by President Johnson in 1968. The winner of Anacin's all-expenses-paid Holiday in Europe grand prize didn't have to worry. Second prizes in the "Holiday from Headaches" promotion: five 1968 Mercury Cougars. Airline food (inset) was a real meal in 1968.

Always popular with Westerners and horseback riders, blue jeans were hot in 1968. Levi-Strauss sold millions and profits were invested in new lines, such as Mr. Levi's Sta-Prest dress slacks (inset). A perfect car for the long distances out West was Mercury's 1968 Park Lane hardtop with swept-back roof.

Touring golfers pulled out of the Professional Golfers' Association, in 1968, and formed the American Professional Golfers group. Billy Casper won six of the year's tournaments and became the third man in history to net $200,000 in one year. The 1968 Oldsmobile four-door sedan could hold six big winners.

Debra Dene Barnes was picked as the winner of the Miss America Beauty Pageant for 1968. A handsome, young actor named Paul Newman (inset) wanted to become the "Mr. America" of politics. He backed Eugene McCarthy for president. The 1968 Oldsmobile Cutlass was another beauty, with its handsome good looks.

A significant addition to the special-interest car field was the original Hurst/Olds. It was an early "after-market" specialty model. Hurst Performance Products Company started with a new Oldsmobile Cutlass coupe and added many performance and appearance items to make a totally new car.

Drag racing was a growth industry in the 1960s, and a test-bed for the Hurst/Olds. This association was successful for both companies involved and lasted through the 1980s. The name was last used for a $1,500 dress-up kit offered, through dealers, for 1988 Oldsmobiles.

Government figures showed more than 150 million people traveling by air in 1968. Few flew in hot air balloons, like this 1968 Plymouth Satellite owner. Commercial airlines averaged 13 new jets, every 10 days, throughout the year. The Boeing 737 (inset) went 580 miles per hour and held up to 130 passengers.

Double-breasted sports coats and suit jackets were fashionable in mens wear for 1968. This may have been related to the nation's "war mode," as such garments had a military look. The 1968 Plymouth Fury had a look all its own. Last year's new styling was updated with a revised grille and rear end.

In college football, Penn State defeated Kansas by a single point to take the Orange Bowl, while it was Arkansas over Georgia 12 to 2 in the Rose Bowl. Ohio State was Big Ten champion and, in the Ivy League, Yale and Harvard fought to a tie. High school football was big enough to make it into a 1968 Firebird ad.

Lee Travino won $30,000 in the United States Open. South Africa's Gary Player took the British Open and won $50,000 by defeating Bob Goalby in the World Series of Golf. Big purses were related to golf's popularity on television screens (like this Admiral "Jameson" models' big 20-inch screen). Despite big money, some golfers preferred the small, sporty 1968 Firebird 400.

California, land of swimming pools, spawned 1968's best swimmers. In addition to Sacramento's Debbie Meyer, there was Claudia Kolb and Mark Spitz, of the Santa Clara Swim Club and Michael Burton and Zachary Zorn, of the University of California, Los Angeles. Pontiac's 1968 GTO looked great beside a pool.

Several historic auto personalities passed away in 1968. Scottish race driver Jimmy Clark perished in a April 7 crash. Diesel developer Clessie Cummins died August 18 and Volkswagen maker Heinz Nordhoff met his maker April 12. Historic car shows were catching on and Pontiac's 1968 Bonneville had a vintage look.

1969

Men on the moon, the Charles Manson murders, "Oh! Calcutta!" and "Easy Rider," Woodstock and the "Miracle Mets." This was 1969, the year that the "generation gap" hit America. The "boomer babies" of postwar America had come of age. They were struggling for changes in attitudes, society and the world. In colleges across the country, 292 major protests against war and social and racial injustice erupted. Student "radicals": shocked their parents into a slow awareness of the need for a new world order. The "Age of Aquarius" had arrived. It was truly the best of times ... and the worst of times.

World events included Charles DeGaulle's resignation in France; ex-Milwaukee, Wisconsin school teacher Golda Meir's rise to power in Israel and Yassar Arafat's election as Palestine Liberation Organization (PLO) chief. Colonel Moammar al-Qadhafi took control in Libya, while African nationalists fought the Portuguese. El Salvador, Honduras, Brazil and Bolivia were hot spots closer to home. Pakistan's ruler resigned and a military government took over. In Vietnam, Ho Chi Minh "packed it in" by dying in Hanoi, on September 3.

Former President Eisenhower died in Washington, while Mary Jo Kopechne was killed after Senator Ed Kennedy's car overturned in Massachusetts. It was the year of another big rock fest, this one in Altamont, California. (The mini-Woodstock held here, in Iola, Wisconsin, didn't arrive until 1970). Hippies held "love-ins" and "be-ins." Drug abuse became an ugly part of the generation gap, as America's youth pushed experimentation with all aspects of life to the "max."

There were some positive notes in 1969. With American casualties in Vietnam approaching 40,000 deaths and 250,000 injuries, President Nixon began withdrawing troops. About 60,000 were pulled out by year's end. A fairer "lottery" style draft system was put into effect on December 1. In Helsinki, Finland, the long-awaited Strategic Arms Limitation Talks (SALT) conference between the United States and the Soviet Union began.

Young music lovers were singing "Lay Lady Lay," "Leaving on a Jet Plane" and "Honky Tonk Women" in 1969. Television debuts included "The Glen Campbell Show" and "Love, American Style." Movie hits were "Midnight Cowboy," "I Am Curious (Yellow)" and "Chitty Chitty Bang Bang." The latter featured a stylized antique auto named for a trio of historic British racing cars from early in the century.

"Play It Again Sam," "Oh! Calcutta!" and "Promises, Promises" were Broadway hits. Books of the year included *The Godfather*, *Portnoy's Complaint*, *The Andromeda Strain* and *Slaughterhouse Five*.

The nearest thing to the death of an "automotive personality" during 1969, was the passing of writer Jack Kerouac, who barreled a Hudson across the country in his book "On the Road." Aviation pioneers Claude Daynier and Allan Lockheed also passed away. The entertainment world lost Judy Garland, Jeffrey Hunter, Boris Karloff, Robert Taylor and Sonja Henie (the ice skater turned actress). Departing from the world of sports, past and present, were fighter Rocky Marciano and baseball greats Don Hoak, "Lefty" O'Doul, "Red" Rolfe and "Bubbles" Hargrave. Congolese statesmen Joseph Kasavubu and Moise Tshombe both died, as did newspaper columnist Drew Pearson, labor leader John L. Lewis, Senator Everett Dirkson, architect Walter Gropius and Allen W. Dulles, the spark plug behind formation of the Central Intelligence Agency.

The 1969 AMC Rogue hardtop had a bit of the Rebel in it. So did many women that year. Firsts for females included jobs as jockeys, baseball umpires and the president of the United Nations General Assembly. A 21-year-old Irish militant, Bernadette Devlin, was elected to Britain's Parliament, but soon faced prison.

Dresses with bold floral prints and large, antique gold jewelry were in vogue during 1969. Mink stoles were seen less, however. A car not seen much, that may have warranted more attention, was the classy-looking 1969 AMC Ambassador four-door sedan.

The nation's new president, Richard M. Nixon, was an avid golfer. Orville Moody, 35, was the golfer who won the 1969 U.S. Open at the Championship Golf Club, in Houston, Texas, on June 14, 1969. A 14-year army veteran, Moody was mostly unknown. More easy to recognize was the 1969 Buick Riviera Sport Coupe.

America's leading 1969 female tennis players were Mrs. Billie Jean King, Nancy Richey and Julie Heidman. One of the nation's leading muscle cars was the racy 1969 Buick GS 400 Sport Coupe. It featured a new grille, a functional hood air scoop, dual paint stripes and an air cleaner equipped with dual snorkels.

The 1969 Buick Skylark four-door hardtop had a longer wheelbase than two-door Skylarks. This kind of uniqueness and variety seemed to fit well in a youth-oriented society where "do-your-own-thing" was the theme for an entire generation of disenchanted youth.

This 1969 Buick LeSabre convertible was photographed at an oceanside locale. The first man to row across the Atlantic Ocean was John Fairfax, of Great Britain. He completed a 180-day, 4,000-mile voyage from the Canary Islands to Hollywood Beach, Florida in a 22-foot rowboat called "Britannia."

A rapid increase in food prices occurred in 1969. It made the restaurant meal this couple is eating more expensive. Fortunately, earnings were up, too. Americans' per capita income ($3,134) broke $3,000 for the first time. First choice among luxury car buyers was a 1969 Cadillac, like the Coupe DeVille.

In thoroughbred racing, Arts and Letters lost the Kentucky Derby and the Preakness, but won all the other important races to become "Horse of the Year." Barbara Jo Rubin, a new female jockey, took Brave Galaxy to a victory at New York's Aqueduct Race Course. The front-wheel-drive 1969 Cadillac Eldorado was a champion automotive "steed" in its own right.

278

"Marry me! Marry me!" was the name of Claude Berri's 1969 foreign language film. It focused on a mixed-up youth on the brink of getting married. A Spidel watch (inset) could really be a big help in "getting the groom to the church in time." The 1969 Fleetwood Brougham was well-suited for formal occasions.

According to one source, the spring of 1969 brought out some of the handsomest pant suits in neutral colors. General Motors put the Corvair in "neutral," after Ralph Nader's book **Unsafe At Any Speed** *effectively killed its future. This 1969 Corvair Monza Sport Coupe was among the last of the breed.*

Families were shrinking! By the end of 1969, the average American family had 3.1 people, versus 3.3 in 1960. Assuming he's married, this young dad better use his Kodak Instamatic camera (inset) to capture all four kids on film, before 2.7 of them go away. All could easily fit in his 1969 Chevy II Nova, though.

Sharp differences in young and old values, in 1969, created a gulf in understanding tagged a "Generation Gap." Sociologist Margaret Mead said this new phenomena stemmed from absorption of rapid changes in a short period of time. The 1969 Chevelle SS-396 was a world apart from early economy models.

Bell Telephone developed the Code-Com Set in 1969, a telephone that blinked or vibrated, in code, allowing the deaf, dumb and/or blind to communicate. Phones had a fun side, for kids hanging out by a 1969 Camaro SS/rs coupe. Another 1969 communication device was the Zenith portable television (inset).

Orenthal James Simpson was better known as "O.J." In addition to promoting sales of the 1969 Chevrolet Caprice coupe, with his wife Marquerite, Simpson was a halfback for the University of Southern California in 1967 and 1968. The latter year, he won the Heisman Trophy for best college football player.

This 1969 Impala Custom Coupe was a "hit" at the weekly softball game. Softball originated in Chicago, Illinois in 1887. Today's game was developed by Lewis Rober, of Minneapolis, Minnesota. The United States Slo-Pitch Softball Association was formed in 1969. By 1985, it had about 60,000 registered teams.

If this guitarist is singing the 1969 hit "Rain Drops Keep Falling on my Head," he doesn't have to worry about getting wet with his straw hat. Guitarist Glenn Cambell had a new show you could watch on an Admiral console television (inset). However, driving a 1969 Corvette Stingray was more fun.

Jet-like performance was available in the 1969 Corvette Stingray. America's fleet of light planes, including business jets, jumped by more than 13,000 in 1969. That brought the total to 125,000. On October 31, a marine corporal hijacked a TWA commercial jet from California to Rome, Italy in the first transatlantic skyjacking.

Grand Canyon National Park, in Utah, and Scotts Bluff National Monument, in Nebraska, observed 50th anniversaries in 1969. All told, attendance at National Parks rose 7.9 percent. For those who liked visiting parks and remote campsites, Chevrolet offered the 1969 Blazer Sport Utility with four-wheel-drive.

Fruit crops had a exceptional year in 1969. Production of all fruits was up: apples (three percent); peaches (three percent); pears (15 percent); and grapes (nine percent). A record citrus crop was still being counted at year's end. The lady of the farm did a fine job hauling crops to market in a 1969 Chevrolet C10 pickup.

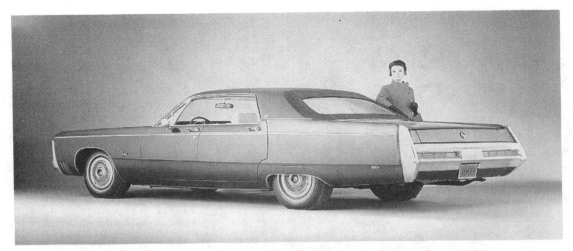

In banking, the Federal Reserve Board hiked the prime rate to 8.5 percent on June 9, to help control inflation. A high level of economic activity and steep demand for credit dominated this industry. At $5,770, a car with a lot of appeal to bankers (and their wives) was Chrysler's 1969 Imperial four-door hardtop.

In 1969, bricklayers earned $5.85 per hour, factory workers averaged up to $3.23, and retail clerks came in between $2.76 and $3.20. Most of them were not in the market for the high-priced Imperial, but Chrysler might be able to sell them a rich-looking 1969 Newport Custom four-door hardtop for $3,730.

Industrial production rose from a 168.7 index in December 1968 to 174.6 in July 1969. A model aimed at the factory owner, who may have been ready for a new car after counting profits at midyear, was the sporty-looking 1969 Chrysler 300 two-door hardtop. It listed for $4,104.

The "General Lee" was one of the stars of the hit television series "The Dukes of Hazard." This series appeared on CBS-TV during the 1970s (?) However, the cars (there were more than one) featured were 1969 Dodge Chargers. They were painted bright orange and had a Confederate flag painted on top.

Tom Wopat (left) played Luke Duke and John Schneider (right) played his cousin Bo Duke. Ben Jones played the role of their friend "Cooter," who cannibalized junk cars to keep the General Lee running after numerous crashes. More than a dozen cars were required, as the stunts in the series often required specially modified stand-ins.

News photos of the Woodstock Music and Art Festival showed young people riding through the streets of Bethel, New York on the hoods of automobiles. The famous August 15-17 event drew 300,000 youths to the small upstate hamlet for an outdoor rock festival. This model is perched on the hood of a 1969 Dodge Dart Swinger.

Young designers like Mary Quant and Rudi Gernreich pushed "do-your-own-thing" fashions. Mini-skirts rose higher than ever in 1969, often accompanied by the "bra-less" look. This gent may feel his lady friend revealed too much and draped his sport coat over her. His 1969 Dodge Charger R/T was also "too much" in a good sense.

The United States population, in 1969, included 78.5 million people up to 19-years-old; 42.6 million 20- to 34-year-olds and 35.2 million 35- to 49-year-olds. For men, the popular "Mod" look often included a bush or safari jacket and bell bottom jeans. The 1969 Mustang two-door hardtop also had a stylish, modern appearance.

This woman seems like she's looking for someone to race against her 1969 Mustang Sportsroof (Ford's term for fastback). These cars were very competitive in the Sports Car Club of America's popular Trans-Am sedan-racing series. In open-wheel auto racing, Mario Andretti earned $805,127 by winning the Indy 500.

Pony cars retained "Walter Mitty" appeal for middle age and up men, They comprised a large market. The "older middle age" bracket included 29.6 million Americans 50- to 64-years-old. The 65-years and older category represented 19.6 million citizens. Still, a Shelby GT-350 convertible was more of a youth machine.

The Theory of Flight for Gliders (second edition), by R.C. Allen, was printed in 1969 and remains a leading reference for sailplane enthusiasts. Most of these aerodynamic aircraft, built with modern technology, will soar on all but the calmest days. A car that soared into the hearts of 1969 buyers was the Ford XL Sportsroof.

"The Wall" was a term people associated with divided Germany in 1969. Of course, Berlin's barrier didn't look like the brick wall behind this 1969 Ford Fairlane 500 convertible. During the year, the 20th anniversary celebration of East Germany was held in East Berlin and German Communists made friendly overtures to the West.

Ford Motor Company used a digital computerized Hydraulic Ride Simulator to test the road characteristic of cars like this 1969 LTD two-door. Another digital computer system developed in 1969 generated television displays of the moon's surface for training astronauts. It was called the Lunisim system.

A "moon roof" option for the 1969 Thunderbird two-door Landau seemed most fitting. This was the year that man first stepped on the moon. In May, three astronauts flew a lunar module within 10 miles of the lunar surface. Then, in July, three others went back. At 10:56 pm (EST) on July 20, Neil Armstrong walked on the moon!

You could carry 12 people in Ford's new, 1969 Club Wagon . The company advertised it as "the roomiest wagon ever built." Its smooth-riding Twin-I-Beam independent suspension made it a comfortable people-carrier, too.

The Bureau of Outdoor Recreation, established in 1962, was provided $94.3 million in the 1969 budget to acquire 275,600 acres of federal recreation lands and waters. That news probably made this hunter very happy. He would soon have more good hunting spots to challenge his 1969 Bronco's go-anywhere abilities.

A 1969 Ford Camper Special was great for trips. The 100th year since John Wesley Powell's trip down the Colorado River via the Grand Canyon, was marked at Glen Canyon National Recreation Area (Utah) on June 19, Dinosaur National Monument (Utah) on June 26 and Grand Canyon National Park (Arizona) on August 16.

Some people are proud of their pets and dress up to show them off. These folks had a pet collie and a pet 1969 Lincoln Continental. Axer Patzwald was proud of Top, her Harlequin Great Dane. He won Ken-L-Ration's 1969 dog of the year medal for pushing a girl from the path of a truck and bringing aid to a second, drowning child.

Residential outlays, in 1969, hit $29.95 billion, up four percent from 1968. New housing accounted for $23.4 billion, a five percent jump. Work began on about 1.5 million new homes. A four percent decrease was blamed on tight money. This couple was loose enough with money to buy a 1969 Lincoln Continental two-door hardtop.

Expenditures for home and property improvements leveled off at $5 billion in 1969. That total may have included work on this gentleman's home or lawn. Both were certainly huge. So was his 1969 Continental Mark III. The domestic sub-compact did not arrive until the spring of 1969, when Ford introduced its 1970 Maverick.

What could be better to go with a massive house and 1969 Lincoln Continental Mark III, than a new Admiral Duplex freezer/refrigerator (inset)? As well as 16 cubic-feet of food storage, this appliance featured automatic door closers, easy-roll wheels, an ice-cube maker, a tilt-out juice can dispenser and a roll-out frozen food basket.

In 1969, the Bureau of Public Roads managed a Traffic Operations Program designed to make better use of existing roads by increasing the capacity of streets in urban areas. It used traffic engineering techniques, rather than costly construction. Moving down the road in a small city is a 1969 Mercury Cougar convertible.

Shifts, like the one on this 1969 Mercury Montego owner, were still worn over swimsuits. The United States remained dominant in competitive swimming. Americans set four of the year's nine new men's swimming records and two of three women's marks. Gary Hall, Mark Burton, Susie Atwood and Debbie Meyer starred.

This trailer pulled by a Mercury Monterey had several new National Park System areas to visit in 1969. They included the Marble Canyon monument in Arizona, the Lyndon B. Johnson historic site in Texas, the Florissant Fossil Beds monument in Colorado, and the Saint Croix scenic river between Minnesota and Wisconsin.

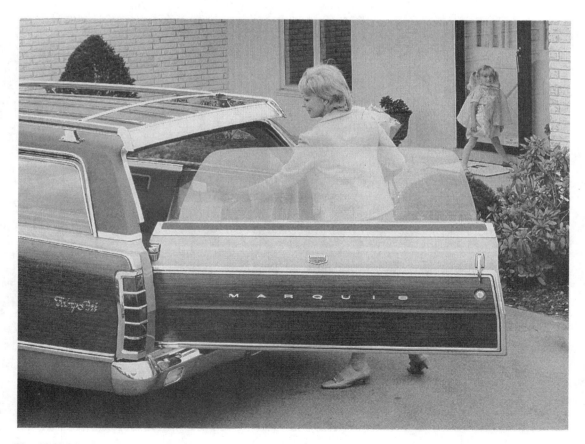

The 1969 Mercury Marquis station wagon offered a new "Dual-Action" tailgate that dropped down or swung out on hinges. The side-opening feature was more convenient for shoppers. While her mother unloads the groceries, this young lady heads towards the television with a huge bag of Lays potato chips marked 79-cents.

*Was it coincidence? Irving Schulman published his book **Valentino** in 1967 and, two years later, Oldsmobile compared the quiet muscle of its 1969 Ninety-Eight Sport Coupe to the strong, silent characters that Rudolph Valentino portrayed in silent films like "The Sheik" (1921) and "Son of the Sheik" (1922).*

*The 1968 book **Kops and Custards: The Legend of Keystone Films**, was written by Katon C. Lahue and Terry Brewer. Mack Sennett had the idea for zany cops at Keystone Films in 1912. The seven originals bowed in 1914, lead by Ford Sterling. This ad related the fun of driving a 1969 Oldsmobile "88" to the fun of watching silent film comedies.*

Three Western films were 1969 box office hits: "The Wild Bunch," "Butch Cassidy and the Sundance Kid" and "Paint Your Wagon." Oldsmobile joked that 1969 Vista Cruiser wagon buyers could "keep a sharp lookout" for outlaws. The new West, characterized by the Astroworld amusement park in Houston, (inset) was changing.

There were record snowfalls in the Midwest during the winter of 1968-1969. The United States Weather Bureau issued long-lead-time forecasts of potential flooding that mitigated disasters in the spring. The front-wheel-drive 1969 Oldsmobile Toronado was an excellent "snowmobile."

The Road Runner, a bird found in Southwestern states, such as Arizona, is one of 127 species of cuckoos. It is known as a poor flyer. However, the 1969 Plymouth Road Runner Sport Coupe could really fly. With a 383 cubic-inch V-8, it could do the quarter-mile in just over 15 seconds.

Project Stormfury was a joint program of the Environmental Science Service Administration, the U.S. Air Force and the U.S. Navy to investigate Hurricane modification. Hurricane Debbie was successfully seeded twice, with the results to be analyzed later. Another "storming" success was the 1969 Plymouth Fury.

Robert Redford had a surprise hit in his 1969 film "Downhill Racer," a beautifully filmed ski story. Pontiac's GTO was named official car of the United States Ski Team that year. Another fun winter machine was the 1969 Ski-Doo (inset). Made by Bombardier, Limited, it was North America's best-selling snowmobile.

"Cactus Flower," starring Walter Matthau, was one of a number of plays and musicals that moved directly from Broadway to summer theater in 1969. This hadn't been the trend with stage productions for several years. A real flower of the desert, or any other region, was the redesigned 1969 Pontiac Grand Prix.

Going out to eat, in 1969, rarely meant grabbing burgers at MacDonald's. Less than 32,000 fast food outlets existed that year, compared to 90,000 in 1988. While this couple may have eaten "slow" food, they owned a fast car. Their 1969 Pontiac Bonneville four-door hardtop came with a standard 428-cubic-inch V-8.

Money made news in the art world. California's Norton Simon Foundation spent a record $550,000 for a Degas' pastel and Christie's sold a Gauguin self-portrait for $313,953 in Geneva. A Rembrandt portrait fetched $756,000 in London. At $3,625, Pontiac's artistic-looking 1969 Bonneville was bargain-priced.